Great North of Scotland Railway

Ideal Winter Resorts

	Height above sea level. Feet.
BANCHORY	200
ABOYNE	410
BALLATER	660
BRAEMAR	1100

SKI-ING . .

SKATING . .

CURLING . .

GOLFING . .

BRACING AIR

Convenient Train Service to and from ABERDEEN in connection with SOUTH Trains

Motor Omnibus Service between BALLATER and BRAEMAR

Travel Information from:—

PASSENGER SUPT., 80 GUILD ST., ABERDEEN
EDINBURGH OFFICE . . 29 HANOVER ST.
GLASGOW OFFICE . . 42 ST ENOCH SQ.

ABERDEEN   GEORGE DAVIDSON, *General Manager.*

"SKISTERS"
The Story of Scottish Skiing
by MYRTLE SIMPSON

"Watch out"
Allan Arthur warned the
Scottish Mountaineering Club

"or you may well go down
with a bad attack of ski fever
which I question if
even Father Time will cure"

"SKISTERS"

The Story of Scottish Skiing

by MYRTLE SIMPSON

LANDMARK PRESS, CARRBRIDGE, INVERNESS-SHIRE

First published, 1982
Landmark Press, Carrbridge, Inverness-shire
© Myrtle Simpson

Designed by George Nicol, Edinburgh

ISBN 0 9503440 1 X

This story has been compiled with assistance from many quarters. The Journals of the Scottish Ski
Club, Dundee Ski Club and Aberdeen Ski Club have been an important source of reference as have
the early editions of the Cairngorm Club Journal, Scottish Mountaineering Club Journal and the Ski
Club of Great Britain Year Book.

I am particularly indebted to the following for information on the early days of Scottish skiing:
Bob Clyde, Frith Finlayson, Brigadier Sir John Forbes of Allargue, Karl Fuchs, Lt. Col. J.P. Grant of
Rothiemurchus, Chris Lyon, L.R.S. Mackenzie, Roddie MacLean, Philip Rankin, William Spiers,
Dick West, and Rev. J.S. Wood.

Much help was received from Mrs. Aline Dunlop, the daughter of Allan Arthur, who made her
father's diary available, and the Misses MacRobert who allowed access to their father's photograph
albums. In addition George Stewart combed the archives of the Ski Club of Great Britain for
reference to Scotland. Mary Currie, Jean Stewart, Robert Benzies and Mike Kenneth gave freely of
their time. The latter also allowed me the unlimited use of his extensive photographic collection.

Myrtle Simpson, 1982

Frontispiece Toiling up Ben Dubhchraig, 1912.
(H. MacRobert)

Printed by Nevisprint, Fort William

CONTENTS

1. FLEETING BOARDS

There was fresh snow on the hills on the 12th March 1892. W.W.
Naismith and a friend boarded the train in Glasgow for Kirkintilloch,
then caught the early trap to Milton of Campsie. Bystanders were
surprised to see them shouldering long heavy planks of wood and setting
off to clamber up to the snow behind the village.

The wooden planks were ash skis, seven feet long and four and a half
inches wide with leather fastenings. The young men fixed the straps over
their heavy workmen's boots and skied up onto the ridge before
following the crest for two miles to a top known as the Meikle Bin. It
was a clear crisp spring day and the two men were thrilled with the
view. The hills were glistening white, the sun sparkling off the fresh
snow. Naismith could see right across Scotland, from the Ochils and
Firth of Forth to the Arran hills beyond the Clyde. They retraced their
tracks, and Naismith found that a very slight gradient was sufficient to
set the skis sliding at a tremendous speed. As the angle steepened, he
kicked them off and sat on them instead, turning the skis into a
toboggan. He could hardly wait till the next annual dinner of the
Scottish Mountaineering Club to relate his experience.

A love of the countryside was a new concept in Victorian Europe.
People previously had had little admiration for the wild and picturesque,
but now the industrial revolution had filled the towns with smoke and
noise. To escape from the sprawling cities, the intelligentsia began to
search for space, peace and adventure – and found it in the hills. As a
result of this interest thirty gentlemen had gathered in the Grand Hotel,
Glasgow at 6.15 p.m. on March 12th 1889 – solicitors, doctors, bankers,
businessmen and a few ministers of the church. They had come together
to consolidate the Scottish Mountaineering Club. Professor G.C.
Ramsay of Glasgow University, took the chair. His brother had made
the first ascent of Mont Blanc from the Courmayeur side in 1854, and
was a founder member of the Alpine Club. Professor Ramsay recognised
that the greatest charm of the hills lay in peace and solitude but felt that
an association of men with a common interest would benefit all.

After a business meeting and a hearty dinner of duck, Professor
Ramsay pushed back his heavy mahogany chair and rose to address the
gathering. He reminded them that the Club had been formed with the
aim of broadening their love of the mountains through the purchase of
maps, the exchange of information concerning weather and as a means
of approaching landowners for the use of bothies and access to the hills.

It was due to W.W. Naismith that this gathering had been called. He
worked in a Glasgow office but hated the tedium and longed for space
and adventure. He read every account of travellers' discoveries and
yearned to be an explorer, but had to be content with the nearby hills.
Every Sunday he walked to the Campsies or Kilpatricks, returning in
time for evening service at Hyndland Church, where he later became an
elder. He was not completely alone on the hills and friendships sprang up
among those whom he met on the way.

Stimulated by accounts of the Arctic, Naismith particularly loved the
winter months. His new friends though, were reluctant to join him
when there was snow on the ground. They felt afraid and unable to
handle the difficulties. Naismith urged them to master conditions in the
hills all the year round. He felt so strongly on this point that he put it to
the Club that the 10/6d. entry fee of new members should not be
accepted until they had proved their ability to ascend the Scottish hills in
snow.

When the translation of Nansen's account of crossing Greenland on
skis in 1888 reached Glasgow, Naismith read it with tremendous
excitement. He saw at once that the ability to ski opened up undreamed
of possibilities. Instead of plodding up a few miles of snow covered
slopes, he could venture right into the heart of the hills.

At the next meeting of the Mountaineering Club, Naismith gave an
account of his day on Meikle Bin and pointed out to members that with
skis they could range all over Scotland even in winter. He explained to
them that the snow "skates" as used in Northern Europe and Asia cost
£1. However, he had found that it was possible to obtain them for a few
shillings if ordered direct from Messrs. Hagen and Co. of Bergen, who
would deliver them to Leith. He also informed the Club that the correct
pronunciation was "shee" and that the one word was also the plural. He
concluded his account by mentioning that the skis were not of much use
on the ascent, but on level ground or on soft snow, better progress was
made with them than without. "Skis might often be employed with
advantage in winter ascents in Scotland", he said. "And in the Alps it is
not unlikely that the sport may eventually become popular, particularly
with a blasé climber."

Naismith was right. By 1893 the Alpine Journal reported that skis

8

were for sale in several London shops and would make an ideal Christmas present. Harold Raeburn, though, bought his in Norway and during the winter of that year carried them out from his home in Edinburgh and ascended the Blackford hill, the Braids and even crossed several of the Pentland passes. "However," he wrote in the Scottish Mountaineering Club's Journal, "as far as my opinion is concerned the ski will but seldom be used in Scotland with advantage and enjoyment." Raeburn came to this conclusion after many days of unsuitable snow in and around Edinburgh. In a letter to the Club president, he dismissed Naismith's enthusiasm as there were often winters with no snow at all in the neighbourhood of Edinburgh and Glasgow and he could not imagine travelling any further afield.

In February of 1895 upper Donside was paralysed with snow drifts blocking the roads and cutting off crofts and castle alike. Dr. Howie, a Cypriot by birth, was the local G.P. His scattered practice included the Forbes family at Castle Newe. The laird's young wife was expecting her first child, and as the pregnancy was threatening complications, Dr. Howie had advised her to stay quietly in bed. Lady Emma had followed this advice, but preferred the family's shooting lodge at Delnadamph to the castle. Now the baby was due, but Dr. Howie realised that his patient was still at the lodge, cut off by snow, three miles up the Glen beyond Cockbridge. He collected skis from the castle and set off for the lodge. He covered the last three miles in four hours but arrived in time to successfully deliver the baby girl.

It was not however until some years later that people ventured into the real mountains of Scotland for sport. In 1904, a friend of Naismith's, J.H. Wigner, described in the club's journal, how he ascended Ben Chonzie in the spring: "Train to Crieff – by 10 a.m. clear of the village and walked at fair pace towards Loch Turret. Ski on just below loch, and in five minutes on unbroken snow. Up steep slope, necessitating many zig-zags, to summit ridge, arriving 1 p.m. at first cairn, 2,571 feet. Magnificent shoot down to col between this point and Chonzie – plugged on my hardest up gentle and unbroken snow slopes, arriving 2.25. Descended to col in four minutes! and reached starting point in $1\frac{1}{2}$ hours. Snow throughout day in ideal condition, and hills perfect for ski-running."

Alpine skiing was meanwhile developing fast. In 1888 a Colonel Napier produced the first pair of skis in Davos, and, in the same year Sir Arthur Conan Doyle crossed from Davos to Arosa, describing his adventures in the Strand magazine. He negotiated the steeper slopes by sitting on the skis, and wrote ruefully that the seat of his Harris tweed trousers wore out as a result, in spite of his tailor's confidence that this was impossible.

In the Alps, at the turn of the century, British skiers were carrying out impressive tours, using one stick, strap bindings and ordinary walking boots. Skis were dipped in water so that a thin film of ice would act as a check when climbing. Speed was reduced and a gradual change of direction made by leaning heavily on the one stick. Many skiers reached the Alps under the guidance of the first travel agent, Henry Lunn. He gave his son Arnold a pair of skis in 1898. It was this gesture that led to Arnold's lifelong dedication to the development of skiing. A fellow enthusiast was E.C. Richardson, who founded the Ski Club of Great Britain on 6th May 1903, and was recognised as "the Father of British skiing".

Richardson was, in fact, a Scot, born in Dumbarton in 1871 and educated at St. Ninians, Moffat. Although working in England, he maintained a strong interest in the activities of Scottish climbers and knew most of them well. He often remarked that those who were fortunate enough to be able to remain in Scotland did not make the most of their luck as they seldom went into the hills in winter, or used them as a training ground for higher endeavour in the Alps. These feelings led Richardson to suggest to the Scottish Mountaineering Club that they should devote their Easter Meet of 1904 to learning how to ski. At his instigation, W.R. Rickmers, a German, resident in London, but married to a Scot, travelled to Fort William to join the party of climbers staying at the Alexandra Hotel. He considered skiing "the finest variety of mountaineering" and wrote lyrically on the subject: "Having ascended a hill, who can describe the feelings of the downward slide, the exuberant joy of swaying motion − in short the whole rippingness of a good run? Having partook of our wholesome food at the summit, how we do delight in the view, so deep, so clear, that crystal purity wherein seems to float the promise of eternity. Survey with pride the many windings of the clear cut line of ski tracks − what man-made beauty. ..."

West coast rain poured down on Rickmers and his pupils for four days, as they plodded up the slopes of Ben Nevis, "snatching from driving sleet and cutting wind a few moments of practice on the fleeting boards." They persevered, as Rickmers felt that snow was often at its best in bad weather. His party ate their sandwiches "Where the water seemed most driest" and fended off the cold with tweed and gabardine.

On the fifth day, they were rewarded. The sky cleared and the skiers reached the summit. Steep stretches of unbroken snow fell away below them equalling anything that Rickmers had seen before in the Alps. The proximity of the blue sea mingling with the white mountains was

The "Lilienfeld" binding was favoured by most Scottish skiers.
(Scottish Mountaineering Club Journal)

Opposite. Skisters halt for lunch near Newtonmore. Allan Arthur, second from the left, started climbing, aged 8, with his father in 1892. His job as an electrical engineer took him all over Scotland at all times of the year. (J.R. Young)

incredibly beautiful to his party. Dr. Inglis Clark was one of them, with his wife and daughter as well as Miss MacPherson and a young man, Allan Arthur.

They now all donned their skis and set off down the soft Easter snow, having a 2,000 foot run in fine conditions, to just above the loch at the col. Miss MacPherson could not manage the final turn and came to a stop in the loch itself. Her thick, long skirt hampered her and Dr. Inglis Clark had to help her remove her skis. Summing up his experience of this visit, Rickmers stated that, "The ground and snow is excellent, but the climate extremely discouraging. The only real drawback in Scotland is the question of good approaches and comfortable lodgings close to snow – not insoluble. However, in fine weather, two hours walk to the snowline is a mere nothing to a ski runner. The question for skisters in Scotland is not one of the ground and snow, but rather the sky above."

In spite of the appalling weather, Rickmers placed an advertisement in the following year's Scottish Mountaineering Club journal. It read: "Mr. W. Rickmers offers to teach S.M.C. members and their ladies to ski. Terms: None. Conditions: Enthusiasm and Discipline."

His own enthusiasm was unabated. During his visit to Fort William he had written the following jingle:

"The turbulent swirl, the storm sped whirl on the fall
    with a thumping bump,
And the lightening fling with the elegant swing of a
    well made telemark jump,
The tinkling crash of the jolly good smash that breaks
    the even flow,
Or the sweeping slide as whizzing we glide through the
    drifts of the seething snow."

Interest in skiing continued to grow among climbers. After the Easter meet of 1904 Rickmers presented the Scottish Mountaineering Club with 12 pairs of skis. The skis were of the so-called "Alpine" type, which was short and rigid with a metal plate hinged at the toe and attached to a powerful spring on the ski, termed the "Lilienfeld" binding. Allan Arthur was one of the first to make use of this gift. He said at the time "The sport of skiing has come to stay" and pointed out that mountaineers could best appreciate its charm and exhilaration.

Scottish skiers, or "skisters" as they were called, considered that the ideal snow for the sport was after a heavy fall, then a thaw, followed by a sharp frost and new snow of about three inches. The Scottish Mountaineering Club journal reported that: "On this, one can travel very fast indeed – 30 m.p.h. being quite common. Retaining balance when descending is a matter of altering one's foot position relevant to one another, and to alter direction, lean on the stick thus avoiding troublesome patches of snow that alternate with ice and drift – it is this glorious uncertainty, especially when travelling fast, that makes the sport such an exhilarating one in Scotland.''

Many Scottish climbers were now visiting the Alps during the winter months. They used their skis as a means to move about in the mountains, maintaining that the day's sport was the climb, not the downhill rush. Limited as their technique was, they completed some remarkable ski ascents. These mountaineers found that they now had as much freedom in the winter as in summer. They were beginning to control their skis by adopting the ideas of an eccentric Austrian, Mathias Zdarsky who lived a hermit-like existence near Vienna in a house that he had built himself. Inspired by Nansen's book, he had ordered a pair of skis from Norway but as they came without any instructions, he was forced to develop his own technique, and out of this came the stem turn. Zdarsky was so excited with this new idea that he challenged a party of Norwegians to a downhill race from the summit of Mont Blanc and when this was declined, modified his challenge to a race on a lower slope. However, the Norwegians complained that the course was still much too steep, and that they would all suffer from vertigo. They had never seen a skier who could run under control over such difficult country and under such conditions as Zdarsky. They were eventually persuaded to race and this occasion can be looked upon as the first modern slalom. The course was down an easy slope, but included forty gates arranged one below the other at a convenient distance. Zdarsky had no interest in racing but only used it to demonstrate that the Norwegian type of skiing was unsuited to steep ground. Everyone at his competition who covered the course within a fixed time received a prize.

Allan Arthur was one of the Scots influenced by the new ideas in the Alps. He now used two sticks, one a strong bamboo pole of six feet, with an iron spike and three inch plate at the end, and the other light bamboo with a swivel pigskin basket for support on soft snow. In ascent, he pushed each arm alternately, but for descending, he held both sticks as one, hooking the basket of the lighter over the other, leaning on the single pole to make tight turns. Arthur discarded the new Norwegian idea of small strips of hide fastened to the back of the skis to prevent slipping. Instead, he applied dabs of floor polish, which had the effect of sticking the skis to the snow. On reaching the summit, however, Arthur would rub the polish off with his hand.

Arthur's enthusiasm was typical of the Scottish skiers of the 1900s. All climbers, they would catch the 6.10 p.m. train from Glasgow, arriving at Pitlochry at 9.30 p.m. then catch the 4 a.m. to Kingussie. One February weekend in 1906, "Three skisters set off from the village on skis on a clear, crisp frosty morning, such as to delight one's heart, heading from the Monadliaths. The summit was reached at 1 p.m. Lunch in the blazing sun, but the snow still keen and dry. Ran back down and onto the next top of Geal Carn and continued with many a good run and some Telemark and Christie swings. Returned by the 'Grampian Corridor' train due in town by 9 p.m."

At the Scottish Mountaineering Club Easter meet at Ben Nevis in the following year, Naismith and Arthur carried their skis to the foot of the Tower Ridge and had some excellent running in the corrie, then up to the summit and experienced great skiing right down to the valley by the Red Burn. "Watch out," Arthur warned "or you will go down badly with ski fever, which I question if even Father Time will cure." The skisters were limited to the hills that could be reached by train. This threw them together and during the winter of 1906, several informal meets were held with about a dozen present. It was felt that they would benefit from co-operation, from swapping information particularly about snow conditions, and any new ideas about technique. They resolved to form a National Ski Club for Scotland. A leaflet was sent out to fifty people known to own skis in Scotland, calling a meeting on November 22nd 1907. It was to be held in the Scottish National Antarctic Expedition's room in Surgeon's Hall, Edinburgh. Fourteen men were present and the leading spirit, J.H. Wigner, invited Dr. Bruce to take the chair.

William Spiers Bruce was born in London, in 1867, of Scottish Norwegian parents. He attended Edinburgh University and through meeting scientists from the Challenger Oceanographical expedition to the Antarctic, became interested in the natural history of the Polar regions. His first Antarctic experience was as surgeon on the Dundee whaler Balaena in 1892. On his return three years later, Bruce took charge of the high altitude observatory on Ben Nevis. His belongings were carried up for him on ponies, and included a pair of skis discarded by Nansen, that had turned up at the Dundee docks. Bruce lived in the observatory for a year. He took part in seven further expeditions to the polar regions and then had a chance to lead his own. Mr. Andrew Coats of Paisley put up the money to buy a small Norwegian whaler which was repaired and refitted in Troon. She was renamed the "Scotia" and left the Clyde on November 2nd, 1902. The Falkland Islands were reached in January and the Antarctic Circle crossed in February. They dropped anchor in the South Orkneys for the winter and built a solid stone house on shore, with walls four feet thick. A magnetic observatory

Refreshments inside the Ben Nevis
Observatory Hotel, 1913.
(H. MacRobert)

The hotel in the former Observatory on
the summit of Ben Nevis, 1913. Dr.
W.S. Bruce, first president of the
Scottish Ski Club spent a year in the
Observatory in 1895.
(H. MacRobert)

was set up inside. From here, Bruce and his scientists made many journeys on ski, studying particularly the snowy petrel and white rumped tern. They set out again the following spring and sailed further south in the Weddell Sea. On March 6th, land was seen, at 74 degrees south, undulating and ice clad, rising to a great height and fading in the distant sky. Bruce named this new land after his patron, Andrew Coats, and safely sailed back to the Clyde by July 31st, 1904.

The choice of Bruce as chairman of the new club endorsed the fact that Scottish skiers were both explorers and climbers, using their skis to travel long distances, rather than solely for sport. This emphasis was continued in the choice of Nansen as the first honorary member. He was now Norwegian Ambassador in London and later became Rector of St Andrews University. He and Bruce became friends and often met to discuss plans for the subsequent journeys to the Arctic.

2. THE SCOTTISH SKI CLUB

The founder members of the Scottish Ski Club sat over their cigars in a cluttered laboratory at Surgeon's Hall and discussed the objectives of the new club. They decided that the main intention was to encourage ski running as a pastime and to promote its development in districts where it could be of real value, particularly to gamekeepers, shepherds, rural postmen and schoolchildren. The most practical aim, though, was to set up a weather reporting scheme. People living in hilly areas would telegraph information on snow conditions, and newspapers were to be persuaded to publish bi-weekly weather reports. The skiers hoped that the railway companies would post notices of these conditions in their principal stations.

The new club was also to gather together descriptions of the best places for ski running, with their accessibility from the various centres, as well as information on hotels, and other accommodation. It was to be explained to landlords that through the club, they would have custom at the time of year when previously "their houses were empty". The secretary was to act as intermediary between them and prospective visitors, and so save troublesome correspondence. In return, the hotel keeper should offer a reduced tariff to members of the club during the winter season. Information was also to be gathered on farmhouses, keepers' and shepherds' cottages, some of them at high levels, useful to members who did not object to roughing it. The railways were to be approached for reduced fares, with the idea of a weekend ticket, enabling cross-country expeditions to be made at a reasonable cost. People prepared to help with gathering information were to be issued with postcards and told to be liberal with these as "the club is quite well able to afford the luxury."

Members of the Club came mostly from Glasgow, Edinburgh and Aberdeen. The majority were men; lawyers, doctors, businessmen and bankers. The few women present were their wives and daughters. Soon the plans were in operation, and information gathered and exchanged. Members could obtain a broadsheet with notes such as this:

"Tomintoul, Banff

Situation: A town on the North side of the Cairngorm Mountains without railway. 1,161 feet above the sea.

Accommodation: Gordon Arms Hotel, proprietor, E. Bakewell.

Open all winter. Twenty bedrooms. 7/- a day.

Access: Not easy. In winter, best from Ballindalloch on the Great North of Scotland Railway. 15 miles drive, mail coach daily in winter, fare 3/-. Or via the hills from Grantown, Highland Railway, 14 miles. More liable to be blocked with snow. Trap to hold three persons, 10/-.

Character of country: Undulating grouse moors, covered with heather, and mountains.

Snow: Apparently as much as at any town in the Cairngorms."

In London, meanwhile, the Ski Club of Great Britain was thriving and the first edition of their Year Book stated that: "We wish to draw particular attention in this article to skiing at home. We intend at all times to give the widest publicity ... to skiing in the British Isles, and look hopefully forward to the day the ashboards and their owners will be a comparatively familiar sight on our own mountains." In 1906, the Year Book gave the first reference to skiing in Coire Cas. On February 21st, E. Wroughton ascended Cairngorm, and on the way down, "by great good luck, hit on the head of this easy gully." He and his friend, Winfield, had brought a spare pair of skis with them to Kingussie on this occasion, "and with these and some others that we made, after the continental manner, with barrel staves from the nearby distillery, we conducted several classes on a hill near Kingussie, which were well attended. Many adults and boys soon showed considerable skill ... The manager of the local distillery complained later that the children had inundated him with requests for barrel staves."

This enthusiasm prompted a local joiner, S. Stewart of Kingussie, to start making skis using pitch pine, as ash was not available, of seven feet eight inches long. He was filled with "the ambitious prospect of establishing himself as the first ski maker in Great Britain." The Year Book carried an advertisement for the Duke of Gordon Hotel, Kingussie which was "splendidly suitable for ski running." At the general meeting of the Ski Club of Great Britain it was proposed that there should be a competition called: "The Championships of the British Isles, and which should be held somewhere in Great Britain ... and open to all British subjects."

Interest in Scottish skiing was now aroused among the Alpine enthusiasts in England and the Ski Club of Great Britain included "Scottish notes" in their annual review. In this, areas for good skiing were identified and readers were invited to write for information to Dr. Wigner, at Dundee University. He recommended the Central Highlands as offering "undoubtedly the best fields, being easily accessible by railway." The importance of access by rail to the snow, led Wigner to write in 1907, "I anticipate that Dalwhinnie, that highest of all the ski centres, will be the ski runner's favourite resort in these islands."

He recommended Newtonmore for grassy, boulder-free, gentle slopes, and Aviemore as the best centre for attacking the Cairngorms, with an approach from the Lairig Ghru. He warned travellers, though, that in 1880 he had been refused food at Coylum Bridge for "breaking the Sabbath". Dr. Wigner pointed out that "ski runners had no difficulty over the question of access in any part of Scotland, with the exception of the Mar Forest. Landowners and tenants have welcomed them and have recognised the fact that no possible damage can be done by skiers in the way of disturbing game or ground."

Lack of accommodation ruled out many of the areas identified as good for ski running, so the members of the Scottish Ski Club decided to erect a club hut. After much argument, it was agreed that Dalnaspidal, on the south side of Drumochter would be the best site. The capital expenditure was expected to be between £100 and £150. It was suggested that friends should be invited to contribute £5 and thus be made a member of the club for life, plus free use of the hut. The building would be of wood, and transferred in sections to the appropriate site, and set up there in a short time. It should have one good sized living room and additional space for hammocks and bunks. A store of groceries would be supplied. Each member using the food would make out his own bill and send the amount to the treasurer. There should be some comfortable basket or deck chairs provided in the hut for the older men who might have lost their taste for "roughing it". Dr. Wigner disagreed with this need as he considered that no skister was old before he was 70! A scale of charges was drawn up – 6d. per day, weekend 3/6d., yearly subscription, 10/-. The Ski Club of Great Britain offered a contribution of £10 for the hut, but in fact, the scheme came to nothing for want of funds.

Club members considered that a tour of 15 to 25 miles was a good day on the hills, particularly for a lady. The Scottish conditions of bare heather, ice and slush however resulted in wear and tear of the skis unprecedented in the Alps or Norway. Allan Arthur recommended rubbing linseed oil into the wood to improve the durability, then covering the sole with solid wax, working it in with a hot flat-iron. On

A single ski stick helps a skister up a slope near Newtonmore, 1911. (H. MacRobert Album)

21

The postman at Braemar used skis
donated by the Scottish Ski Club,
January 16th 1909.
(W. Brown)

Mr. Speedie's wax was available from
1908.
(Scottish Ski Club Journal)

the hill, he considered that a champagne cork was an excellent alternative. It was impossible to buy proper ski-wax in Scotland, so one of the committee experimented with a home-made recipe. After burning five of his family's saucepans, he handed over his results to Mr. Speedy, the chemist at Crieff.

Mr. Speedy perfected the recipe, and by the winter of 1908 his wax could be bought in a solid form as tablets, or a paste in collapsible tubes at 6d. each. The substance was called Speedolin. Members were also advised to carry a potato knife, in order to scrape off the snow and ice that tended to form in the groove of the ski. The knife could be filed to the correct shape at no extra charge if bought from A.B. Foulis, ironmonger, Shandwick Place, Edinburgh.

The Ski Club felt that something ought to be done towards providing skis for use in Highland districts. It was suggested that a small sum, perhaps £10, should be gathered together and spent on a number of skis made locally for distribution among shepherds, rural postmen and children. The idea was followed up and several pairs made at a cost of 10/- each. As a result of a lecture and demonstration by Dr. Bruce, in Aberdeen, the county authority agreed in 1909 to the two postmen of Braemar being issued with skis. These were used with great success on the route to Inverey, so much so that the Post Office proposed to equip other rural postmen in the same way. By the end of the winter, there were ski running postmen in Donside, Speyside and Sutherland.

The postman was not alone on his skis in upper Deeside. The following account appeared in the Cairngorm Club Journal of 1907. "The Arctic character of the winter that has just closed has given ample scope for the enjoyment of the Norwegian sport of skiing without leaving our own shores. On New Year's Day, a friend and I ascended Bennachie from Oyne. We travelled from Aberdeen by the early morning train and managed to strap on our ski in the station and get through the village without any very great demonstration on the part of the inhabitants. The snow was in perfect condition until we got into the wood, but there it became somewhat heavy. We ascended Craig Shannoch, taking slightly longer than a fellow clubman who was on foot, then struck out over towards the Mither Tap. Once on the crest of the hills, we flew downwards, soon reaching the woods of Pittodrie, then dodging in and out among the fir trees, kept on at an immense speed, till we reached a farm about two miles from Pitcaple Station. The good farmer was struck almost dumb at the speed with which we came down the sloping pasture and on our enquiry how long we should take to reach Pitcaple, we were informed that it took 'aboot half an 'oor tae walk, but ye'd gang in aboot twa meenuts on thae things.' However, he

Skisters above Ballater, January 1912. (E.C. Richardson)

underestimated our time as we found that the snow on the turnpike was not in very good condition so our progress was slow. On reaching Pitcaple, we kept on to Inveramsay where we caught a suitable train home." The writer pointed out that he was used to the district when the hills were green, yet in the calm winter's evening, with the daylight flickering, he "found many a charm in the glen which she does not reveal to her summer visitor."

In the Alps, Vivian Caulfeild was an influence on skiing technique. He was the first to understand the dynamics of the turning ski, and developed the stem christie. This was ideally suited to the hard snow and icy ridges of Scotland. The telemark had been adequate for gentle slopes of soft snow, but this new turn could enable a skier to change direction on a wind polished surface at a steep angle.

One of the first Scots to master the stem christie was Colonel Malcolm of Inverness. He found that he could tackle steeper slopes and travel much faster, as he was in control of his skis and could turn where he chose. He also realised that his new ability to move fast through the winter hills could be of use to the army. With this in mind, he imported 12 pairs of skis from Norway and brought his brigade of Territorials from Fort George to Strathspey.

Colonel Malcolm went to the Alps during the following winter, and met the leading English skier, E.C. Richardson. As well as being able to stem christie at speed, Richardson was a keen ski jumper. Malcolm was so impressed with this ability that he invited Richardson to the Easter gathering of the Scottish Ski Club that was held at Aviemore. Richardson considered that the chief value of learning to jump was that it inspired confidence. He wrote that, "In the course of the quick runs, leaps, turns attempted, one learns how to keep cool and collected when travelling at a speed hitherto unapproached and finds that a fall taken when travelling is not a serious matter after all. ... To overcome nervousness practise on a very steep slope. Build the 'take off' high and scoop out lots of snow immediately below it, so as to make it look as alarming as possible, then you go over anyhow and will be surprised how easy and harmless such a dreadful looking thing can be." Richardson spent the five days of the meet skiing with the club on Braeriach, demonstrating the stem christie and leading them over any obstacles rather than round.

Colonel Malcolm was an apt pupil. He felt that Richardson's idea of teaching to ski by jumping was ideal for his soldiers, so, on returning to Fort George he constructed a movable jump of wood. This he erected on the ski slopes above Dalwhinnie and found that all his friends wanted to try it out. On one day of bad weather they had great sport without going

Opposite. A lunch stop on Geal Charn, 1910.
(C.M.J. Tennent)

24

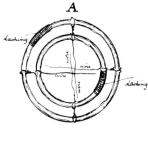

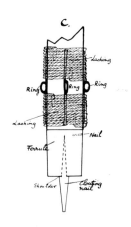

Instructions in the Scottish Ski Club
Journal of 1911 for making ski sticks.
(Scottish Ski Club Journal 1911)

more than a few miles from the village. Appreciating this, Malcolm
urged the Ski Club to erect many more jumps close to all the ski areas so
that they could be used in blizzard conditions.

The Scottish Ski Club realised that in order to develop their sport
long the lines that Malcolm suggested, additional capital was needed.
This could only be achieved if membership was increased. Dr. Wigner
was asked to write a letter to all the leading Scottish and English papers
advocating skiing in Scotland as a "beneficial occupation for mind and
body". In March of 1908 the papers carried a letter extolling the mystery
and challenge to be found in the hills of home. Posters of snow covered
mountains were also erected in the mainline railway stations in England.
People were familiar with outings to the countryside in summer, but to
find pleasure in it in the winter was a new idea.

As a result of these efforts many skiers came north for the first time.
To their surprise, they enjoyed some very good sport. The English skiers
had mostly procured their equipment in Europe, and were astonished to
come across Scots, such as Allan Arthur, using homemade bindings and
sticks. Directions for making these bindings were carried in the Ski
Club's News sheet. "Two steel hinges, each flap one and a half inches,
placed abreast with front flaps screwed down to ski. An eight inch piece
of belting $3^1/_2$ inches broad, rivetted above back flaps (8 inches being
distance from toe to heel of boot).

The outside corners of back flaps cut away to leave space for ends of
toe straps which are rivetted to under side of belting flush with the metal.

Instep straps rivetted to other end of belting. Heel straps rivetted to toe
straps to instep straps. Above the belting under the ball of the foot is
fastened a shorter piece of belting thus raising the toe above the copper
rivets. Under the lower belting, a piece of Dunlop outer tyre is fastened
which, with a longer piece of the same nailed to tread of skis, prevent
clogging underfoot. Total cost, about 1/- per binding.

The fastening is light, is as rigid as I care for and has given no trouble
during two seasons. The hinge allows great length of stride and is less apt
than the more rigid binding to wrench a weak ankle. It may have
disadvantages, though in leaping etc., of which I am unaware. I advise
sticks used in Scotland to be made of hazel as bamboo is likely to split in
our rough conditions, and ash is far too heavy for a double stick."

Information available to the Scottish skier had greatly improved. The
Ordnance Survey now issued a new "one inch" map in five colours,
that covered most of the country. A set of eight cards, giving pictorial
instruction of ski running was also available. These had been compiled
by Richardson for the Ski Club of Great Britain to which the Scottish
club was now affiliated. Weather forecasts were carried by the leading

papers on Friday and Saturday mornings. Members of the two clubs who wanted a special report on snow conditions could receive one by sending a telegram to Dr. Wigner. Edinburgh members could see a report in the windows of either Messrs Anderson of 101 Princes Street, or Lumley's in Leith Street, while Glasgow members had to rely on telephoning their local secretary. All the information for these forecasts had been gathered by the Scottish Ski Club's network of reporters.

Skiers took to the hills dressed in Norfolk jackets, gabardine plus-fours or heavy twill breeches. A notice in the press advised ladies that, as from the autumn of 1911, they could purchase a "two piece woollen Norfolk suit with knickers similar to boys', and a short unlined skirt to be carried in the rucksack for donning before reaching the station or hotel. Women are advised to wear strong leather boots — not to bother with soft, yielding kid — large enough for two pairs of Shetland stockings. Ox leather, size 4 are now available."

Mrs. Inglis Clark was president of the Scottish Ladies Climbing Club. Her skiing had progressed since the Easter of 1904 that she had spent on Ben Nevis with Rickmers. Although an ardent supporter of the Womens' Rights movement, she advised lady skiers not to despise the escort of a man, as his extra strength was a useful standby in an emergency. She, nevertheless, believed in women being self sufficient and urged them to carry their own rucksack with sandwiches and an extra wrap and to have their own knife for scraping icy skis, "My advice to ladies is to commence at once and pass from stumbling beginner to expert to whom the wonderful snow scenes unfold a new page of the world's mystery." They should also carry a length of rope, which they could wind round their ski in a criss-cross fashion, thus preventing slipping backwards on an icy day. "With this one can go straight up a slope as steep as a roof of a house — an invaluable device for cross country skiing, as long as one remembers to slip it off for ski running downhill."

The first account of this new idea being used was in an ascent of Mount Keen, which was reached in six hours from Ballater. Henry Alexander, accompanied by A.J. Butchart of Aberdeen reported that they wound thin rope round their skis before stepping onto the snow. Alexander was amazed to find that he could head straight uphill, without slipping back. Instead of picking a zig-zag route to slowly gain height, the two men headed directly for the summit. Then they found that the knot securing the rope was impossible to untie. Reluctantly, Alexander cut it, cringing at the expense. It was a great day, though: "The hills were one waste of snow, as far as the eyes could see. On foot, we could only have gone a mile or so, as snow too soft to bear one. With ski, however — go anywhere, and on a day like this with snow over valley

56 S.M.C. Easter Meet 1913. Avemo

<u>Cairn Gorm Range Contd.</u>

<u>Cairn Gorm + Ben Macdhui</u> .

(3) Frid . 21st March 1913. On Skis . Avemore
Skis Station Hotel .7·45. Drove to Glenmore Lodge, 9·15
Cairn Gorm 4084' - 12-0/20. Macdhui 4296'..3- 0/5
Lochan Maine .3142' - 4-15/30. Derry Lodge 6-35
N Slopes very wind swept. Bare ridges to top.
S ... plenty of snow.
Summit plateau very icy + dense mist b
3200'. Strong S.SW Gales. Very Cold .
G Sang + Ad on Skis - Fine day. Ski

(2) Club touring test . 16 m. Carried 2 m. 4300'. No roa
Carried 13½ lbs + ice axe. 3½ lbs. Q'hrs. Sop

(1)(1) Meall Dubh Achadh . 3268'. Cairn Ban 3443

(2) Sguran Dubh. 3658'. Saty . 22nd March 1913.
Ski. On Skis with G Sang. Derry Lodge (Inn) 9-
Up Glen Geusachan to E 2400' . 12-55/1-20. Lochan Stuiseach
Dubh Achadh .3-25/30. Level Plateau endless Snow he
Cairn Ban . 4-0/15. Sguran Dubh. 4-45. Loch
Eelan Castle for tea. 6-45/7-15. Hotel 8-75.

(3) Ski Club Tour. 25 m. Carried 7 m. 3800' Road 4-
Carried 13½ lbs + Ice Axe. 3½ lbs. 11 hrs. Glorious da
Views. Soft below 2500. Splendid run off Sguran D

Page from the diary of Allan Arthur.
Note the interest in weight, and the
distance covered. His work gave him
access to areas of Scotland never reached
by other skisters.

Sine Clastie 1913.

Cairn Gorm Range. Contd.:

2) _Braeriach 4248 & Cairn Toul 4241._

Monday 24th March 1913. Aviemore 9-40 am.
via An Lichan to Lower Bothy. 10-0/10. Braeriach. 12-30/45
Cairn Toul. 2-2-15 via ridge + Angel's Peak.
Bothy 4-0/5-30. Drone Howe 6-30.
W.C. Church. Hugh Watson, F. Boggs old. Met on 4248.
3 Marshalls. Arnold Brown. W.G. McAllister. Howard & Beards.
As & McAllister on to Cairn Toul with Howard
& Beards for Derry Lodge & back together to Bothy.
Glorious sunny day. Little mist. Superb
view. New 18" snow from North. Ideal Ski-
ing day — 21 miles. 4600'. 11 hours.
Great Cornices in Garbha bheinn.

Ben Wyvis Range.   Alone from Evanton.
Novar Arms Hotel (Munro) Comfortable. Wed. 26/3/13.
Left 6-30am. Tarphackegan 7.45. Fachdach 3018'. 9-5.
Col 9-25. Carn Gorm 3134'. 9-45. Wyvis. 3429 = 10-15/30
2934 — 10-50. An Cabar. 3106. 11-20/25. Achterneed 1-15.
6¾ hours. 21 miles. 4400'. Grand day — no view.
Much hard snow. Easy going. Much top below Cabar
to Achterneed. Good road from 3m out.

and hill, and sun above, we felt we had the hills at our command. Exhilaration of these great white expanses, the thrill of long coasting runs, with snow whistling beneath the ski – things to remember in the dull city days."

Skiing was becoming popular. Members of the Scottish Ski Club began to feel that their sport was degraded as a result. People were identified as skiers, who had little competence, or experience, of the hills. "There is more to skiing than sliding on a patch of snow close to the railway line," remarked Dr. Wigner stiffly. The committee of the club recognised that skiing involved the acquisition of special skills. They began to document these, and considered a test of competence. This could be used as an entry qualification for membership, and so ensure that new members were proficient and interested in the hills and open country in winter. The committee decided that expeditions made in the Alps should not count as a sign of ability. After much discussion, stringent rules were drawn up that had to be met before a new name would be considered for membership. These related to skiing in Scotland, on the particular conditions of snow only to be met with at home.

Scottish Ski Club Rules

"The S.S.C. touring qualifications will consist of:

1. (a) Five different tours of 15 miles each, ascending at least 3,000 feet in all, or
   (b) Three different tours of 25 miles each, ascending at least 4,000 feet in all, or
   (c) Any longer tours will receive consideration from the committee.
2. Each tour must be completed in one day.
3. A maximum of one fifth of the distance or height allowed to be performed on foot, carrying ski, or on a road.
4. A pack weighing no less than 8lbs. must be carried the whole way.
5. Artificial aids such as seal skin bands may be carried and used.
6. For out and home tours, the furtherest point reached must be at least 6 miles from the start, and that point must be some definite natural feature, such as a cairn or a hilltop. The return must be reasonably different from the out route.
7. For out tours, the distance need not be measured on an airline, but may be between points which can be readily identified on a map.
8. The qualification need not be taken in one season but tours which are to count must be intimated to the committee during the season in which they are made.

Toiling up Ben Dubhchraig, 1912.
(H. MacRobert)

9.   On the last two of (a) and (b) tours, candidates must be accompanied by a reliable witness.

10.   All tours to be performed in Scotland.

Explanatory Notes:

Rule 1:   The 3,000 feet and 4,000 feet are the sum of the ascents of any one tour.

Rule 3:   This is to allow of a candidate carrying ski where there is no snow, either near the start or finish or near the top of a hill which is sometimes bare. A candidate may ski on the road but only for one fifth of the distance.

Rule 4:   For convenience, a candidate may finish his tour at the starting point but he is understood theoretically, to arrive somewhere else, so he must carry luggage. Stones may be used to make up the weight desired, but nothing which may be worn or eaten during the journey will count. That is, the pack at the finish must weigh at least 8lbs.

Rule 6:   The main object of the qualification is to encourage touring and so a candidate should make a point of taking a roughly circular route, at least on out and home tours.

Rule 7:   For example, going from Dalwhinnie to Blair Atholl, the candidate would naturally keep to the crest of the ridge as far as possible.

Rule 8:   Further information as to verification will be communicated to the candidates by the secretary on application."

In 1913 the British Ski Association was formed in London. It was a proprietary concern of Sir Henry Lunn and the shop "Alpine Sports". Expecting enthusiasm, Lunn was surprised to meet opposition from the ski clubs. They felt that the organisation was an attempt to control ski running by a firm of travel agents. As a result of the publicity given to the matter in the press by the Ski Club of Great Britain, opposition appeared in the form of an alternative body, the National Ski Union, of which all the ski clubs in Britain were members. The main object of this new body was to form a bond of union among British ski runners, to encourage the sport and generally to protect its interests. Sir Ernest Shackleton, the Antarctic explorer, was to be the vice president. The new union stated that "it was adamant in making sure that the sport was kept in the hands of those who had no connection with any association in which commercial interests are involved."

In December of 1913, skiers waited expectantly for news of Captain Scott and the outcome of his expedition to the South Pole. To them, the

fact that he took many pairs of skis was a special interest. Amundsen had done the same and attributed his success to the continuous use of them. It was a long wait and when the news did come, it was disastrous. Captain Scott was dead. The members of his expedition had been taught to ski by a Norwegian officer, Lieutenant Tryggve Gran, but according to Scott's diary, the skis caused trouble. "December 16th. It is very difficult to know what to do about the ski. Their weight is considerable and yet under certain circumstances, they are extraordinarily useful. December 18th. Left skis behind and started without them, but then returned and thus lost an hour and a half's marching." And finally, "Ski are the thing and here are my tiresome fellow countrymen too prejudiced to have prepared themselves for the event."

Thus began what the Ski Club journal was to call "the winter of our discontent". Following the declaration of war in Europe, several members of the club suggested forming a corps of military ski runners for service on the continent or even at home, should the necessity arise. It was decided however that the number of men who had the necessary skill and had not, at present, joined up, would be negligible. The club held a small, informal dinner in November of the year, with 18 members present, and little realised that this would be their last for many years to come.

Ironically Scottish Ski Club members were soon coming across well trained Italian troops wearing skis, the Alpini. The feats of this mountain corps made a great impression on an Aberdeen skier, Ian McLaren. He wrote home remarking that he was astounded that they could mount guns at 9,000 feet weighing 11 tons. They were drawn into position by steam tractors or swung by aerial chains calles "filovia". "Oh for one on Lochnagar" wrote McLaren ruefully. He also hankered for one of the mess tins used by the Italians, "the same shape as ours, but deeper with a reserve of spirit at the base, and a spirit lamp, enabling the Alpini to make coffee and heat their wine!" He wrote also that "under the snow the mountains had a peaceful fascination which made the horrors of war inconceivable. The sound of a shell bursting came as a desecration to the sense of rest and calm produced by the blanket of snow." McLaren skied to the summit of Lochnagar on his first leave, strapping on his ash boards at Alltnagiubhsaich. He stated on that occasion that he had seen nothing more beautiful than the view that day, in spite of many visits to the Alps and Canada. He was killed at the Somme.

The Scottish hills however were not completely deserted. Activity was to be seen in some unlikely areas. As sleet swept over the Screal Hill above Kirkcudbright on the night of December 16th 1915, Allan Arthur and his friend G. Sang, crouched behind a sheep fank, searching the

Deep snow near Misty Law,
Renfrewshire, 1913.
(H. MacRobert)

horizon for any flickerings of light. They were on the look out for spies. Strange lights had been seen on the moor and odd movements of small fishing boats had been reported. The Government had approached the Scottish Mountaineering Club for a list of names of available men who could keep watch, or find an explanation for the strange events. The club came forward with four teams of two men each, prepared to stand guard for a week. Arthur and Sang formed one team. They had had to load their supplies onto a sledge and pull it behind them as they skied to a bothy at 1,000 feet and settled in for their watch. Each evening they set off in opposite directions and spent the night covering the moorland overlooking the sea.

3. GESCHMOZZLE

Opposite. Señorita de Alvarez preparing for a telemark turn above Castle Newe, Strathdon, 1930. (Forbes Album)

Returning soldiers found that the Scottish Ski Club had foundered. In 1920, the first edition of the British Ski Yearbook, published by the Federation of British Ski Clubs, carried a notice: "As we go to press, we are asked to state that the Scottish Ski Club is most anxious to find a ski runner resident in Scotland who would act as honorary secretary. It would be a thousand pities if this club, which has a very fine record, was allowed to disappear." Two years later, the Year Book reported that: "The Federation of British Ski Clubs regrets to report that the Scottish Ski Club is still in a state of abeyance and that the North of England Ski Club has been wound up owing to lack of support."

The situation, however, was not without hope. At the New Year meet of the Cairngorm Club, H.S. Butchart, now a Colonel, gave some ski instruction at the back of Glen Cluny Lodge. After he had taught his class the rudimentary steps, a start was made for the higher slopes. "The novices managed to get up with few tumbles, except when short runs were attempted. They afterwards negotiated a very enjoyable slow run down to the col. Snow conditions quite unsuitable." M.J. Robb reported that the meet was generally enjoyed by everyone present. The skiing party saw "quite a variety of wildlife near the road and noticed during the return, a pack of grouse being pursued by an eagle."

Various efforts were made to reactivate the Scottish Ski Club but with so little success that it was finally decided to do nothing more until some really snowy winters might rearouse interest. The subject was again raised during the summer of 1929 and it was determined to make a real effort in the autumn to revive the club. As a result, notices were placed in the *Scotsman* and the *Herald*, calling a meeting in the Scottish Mountaineering Club rooms in Edinburgh in November. About 20 people turned up and G. Sang, the former secretary explained why nothing had been achieved since the war. He added however, that he "was glad to be able to give a good account of the club's finances, there being war loan to the value of £50 belonging to the club and a small cash balance." The meeting decided to ask Dr. W. Inglis Clark to continue as

Colonel Forbes, second from the left, his
wife and sister, and R.N.W. How set off
from Tornahaish, Strathdon, February
16th 1930.
(Forbes Album)

How to carry skis on a saloon car,
illustrations from the Scottish Ski Club
Journal of 1935.

president and a committee of ten was appointed to consider how best to resuscitate the club.

As a first step advertisements were placed in the main Scottish papers and a circular was sent to all previous members of the club. Annual subscriptions were fixed at ten shillings. Weekly snow reports were restarted and reporters appointed at Lix Toll, near Killin, Dalwhinnie, Braemar, and the Spittal of Glenshee. Reports were to be sent to the honorary secretary every Wednesday and then advertised in the *Glasgow Herald* and *Scotsman* on the Friday.

The main contrast with pre-war skiing was the use of the motor car. The war had boosted its development and the 1920s saw the advent of Nuffield and Ford, and the beginnings of the family car. Large areas of Scotland not previously used by ski runners now became accessible. The use of skis during the war had also improved other equipment. Lessons learned from the Alpini resulted in the development of steel edges, skins, waterproof clothing and lightweight tents. Slowly, these items began to appear in shops in Edinburgh and Glasgow. Meanwhile, in the Alps, skiing was being transformed from an aid to winter mountaineering to a sport in its own right. This brought about competitive skiing.

People began to be interested in more than just reaching the summit. They started to consider ways of travelling faster downhill and of racing one another to the bottom of the slope. This was found to be great fun, and surprisingly, the next time they skied, they found their technique improved. Skiers raced "just for the heck of it". A group of friends would come together on the top of a mountain and at a signal, all would take off at once, and head for the designated finish. There were no prepared tracks, no flags, and no rules. The first to arrive was the winner. This mass start was known as a "geschmozzle" because of the mix-ups after the starting signal. An advance on this was a race against the clock, a pure test of speed, over open, alpine terrain. This type of skiing led to Arnold Lunn inventing the slalom competition, which was intended to simulate skiing through woods and around obstacles, so emphasizing the necessity for skill and judgement. Lunn used a two-pole gate, a series of which were set in combination on the hill. The two poles could be set in such a way as to trap the skier who did not look ahead, or have the self discipline to turn on the relevant spot. Lunn initiated a competition between Oxford and Cambridge on January 2nd 1920 and the first modern slalom race a year later. The British Ski Championships included a slalom event in 1923. This interest in competitive skiing led to the formation of the Kandahar Ski Club on January 30th 1924, and the Downhill Only Ski Club in the following year.

Scots names were appearing well up the finishing lists of Alpine races,

The summit ridge of Stob Coire an
Lochan.
(S.M. Musgrove)

Ascending Corronaich from Cairn an
Lochan, above Killin. Harry MacRobert
commented that it was a "dull day …
little snow. Lost club hut". November
1935.
(H. MacRobert)

especially that of C.E.W. Mackintosh. He was said to be potentially the finest downhill racer of his time, although accused of throwing away many races by lighthearted carelessness. He won the Roberts of Kandahar race on four occasions and captained two winning teams in the Anglo-Swiss competition. Harold Mitchell, the son of a Scottish industrialist, came first in the Inferno race, the longest downhill race in the world. Born in May 1900, his enthusiasm had a great influence on the Scottish Ski Club of which he was president from 1932–1949. Other Scots were H.R. Spence, who won the British cross-country championships in 1930, as well as various slalom and downhill races the following year, and W.D.M. Raeburn, who came third in the British Championships in 1929, and was well placed in numerous other races during the next ten years.

Alpine skiers returning to Scotland, found that their ability to race helped them to travel faster and so farther, as they could now turn with confidence on rough terrain. This led to the more daring setting off boldly into country never covered before in winter. Harold Mitchell described a tour of Meall a' Bhuiridh in October 1929: "I woke up to find a perfect autumn day, frozen hard – as I discovered after tussle to start car. Leaves in full autumn war paint made glorious countryside. Rich brown tint of bare ground relieved from monotony by patches of water, shimmering in sunlight. To crown all, hills decked in white. All majesty of winter scene without severity. When I tired of roving from one peak to next, relief to follow across vast moor stretching to Loch Rannoch with Schiehallion standing sentinel in the distance. Strangely enough for Scotland, there was no wind. Far off clouds seemed unwilling to move on. In sunshine, powdery snow thawing. Leaving car at highest point 1,454 feet, I was at the extreme low limit of snow line and able to study Meall a' Bhuiridh with a view to making ascent, from the map it appeared ideal, tackled from east or north east (slopes of these aspects provide best snow conditions in Scotland). Shouldering skis, tramped over gentle slopes sinking deep through carpet of snow into soft heather. Up to knees on treacherous patch of bog – progress fairly steady but began to wonder if ski ascent possible after all, for rocky slopes, quite unfit for skiing, guarded eastern approach. Just below rocks, however, I noticed a wide shelf running north. Reaching this, I travelled round into shallow gully, which was well filled with snow, leading upwards in right direction. I followed, though secretly suspecting it might peter out in mass of rocks. However, fears did not materialise and after one difficult area strewn with rocks, gully flattened out. Rapidly mounting soon at summit – 3,636 feet, alone with my ski. Wind still absent and pleasant to enjoy autumn sunshine while searching in rucksack for sandwiches. On

At the Clach Bharig bothy, en route to Cairngorm. Ronald Higginbotham in light plus-fours. Easter meet of the Scottish Ski Club, Glenmore Lodge, 1935.
(H. MacRobert)

Harry MacRobert looks back at Allan Arthur as they ascend Braeriach during the Scottish Ski Club Easter meet of 1922.
(MacRobert Album)

every side there were hills, Nevis to north dominating all else in that direction. In foreground, Buachaille Etive looked black and forbidding, a sombre intruder amongst a crowd of companions in white. Ridge of Clachlet stood out sharply towering over Lochan Easain. Putting on my skis at cairn, I threaded my way amongst rocks at beginning of gully, wide enough for continuous stems except for short distance near bottom which was negotiated by side slipping. Once or twice, tried a telemark as snow was excellent powder, touched but not spoilt by wind. I found, however, that while stems satisfactory with telemark a tendency for leading foot to break through to ground on rocks beneath making turn very unsteady. Interesting to know whether more weight is put on one foot in telemark than in stem. May merely have resulted from fact that when ground is steep, I always force telemark. After halt beside pool for drink, started on easy slopes. Foundation of soft heather or moss made up for thinning snow. Pleasant continuous running possible. Soon the road in view and able to ski right to where had left my car."

Skiers in Scotland found that they must have at least "two skiing turns in one's bag — a pure stemming turn and a 'lifted stem'." A distinguished Scottish skier pointed out that the main difference between skiing at home and abroad was the lack of light and the fact that he would often find himself skiing in: "Mists so dense as to be able to see but a few yards ahead — hell bedeckt — as it was termed in Switzerland." He warned skiers looking for sport at home that: "Snow slopes in Scotland take on a most puzzling kind of surface glare which defies the most hawk eyed of skiers and reduces the short sighted runner, with moisture on his glasses to a state of dithering funk. The run and crash type of skier will have a thin time in Scotland, because even if the slopes are well covered, caution would be necessary. With uncertain snow, heather, rocks, wind swept ice and all kinds of bunkers placed in the most awkward and trying positions, fast running is mere folly. Seldom in Scotland does the snow justify the speed which is ordinary for one in Switzerland. The most innocent and perfect looking snow slope hides rocks hardly covered by snow and most probably others just beyond to catch the falling skier. The stem turn comes into its own on the lower reaches. In heather, no other manoeuvre is any good. A stem or telemark sticks and one cannot jump around because the effort would drive one's ski deep into the heather roots. This turn consists of just lifting one ski up and placing it in the direction one wishes to go and after putting weight on it, lifting the unweighted ski parallel. As Alpine skiers have never tried heather they do not know how to do this — but once acquired, it often saves several hundred feet of walking down — very tiring stuff." This writer also pointed out that in Scotland, the ridges were windblown. Blue ice predominated and when it did not, waves of driven snow confounded the skier. He described once "coming across a whole hill face looking as if a stormy sea had suddenly become congealed and this and all other kinds of snow were only too common. A hard crust can form and then the ski gets no grip at all, and sliding sideways becomes the only means of descending."

In spite of these difficulties, the Scottish tourers were covering new ground and travelling remarkable distances. They were enthusiastic, and full of excitement as they left their cars and set out across the untracked snow. In 1926, young W.B. Spiers imported a pair of skis from Berne and used them in the early part of the winter, on the Glen Fruin Hills, the Campsie Fells and the Ochils. Later in the season he climbed Meall a' Bhuiridh from Ba Bridge, the Drumochter hills, Cairngorm, Braeriach, Ben Lui, Ben Oss, Beinn Dubhchraig and Beinn Heasgarnich. Professor Burnett of Dumfries preferred the Border hills. In the winter of 1932 he skied for 16 consecutive weekends in the area near the lead mines at Wanlockhead. The local miners' children were so intrigued, that he showed them how to make skis with barrel staves and leather strap bindings. His pupils vanished, however, with the closing of the mines in 1934.

Skiers now gathered regularly together. Allan Arthur, Harry MacRobert, A.F. Wallace, John S. Pitman, W.R. Higginbotham and G.J. Scaramanga, to name but a few. The most popular meets were at Killin where about 70 or 80 skiers would congregate. One complaint of the meets was that, "Mr. Mitchell kept urging us to go faster, whereas the average Scottish skier is desperately trying to find a way to slow down." A hut was erected there in 1932 on the col between Meall Corranaich and Beinn Ghlas above Loch Tay at a height of 2,300 feet, about an hour's walk from the road. The hut had cost £15 and had previously been used as the servants quarters at Luib shooting lodge.

With the collapse of the pound sterling in 1932, some 2,000 people travelled north at New Year in search of snow. The most unlikely places claimed to be winter sports resorts. The railway companies joined in the great "Winter Sports in Scotland" campaign and issued a booklet. The main promotion centred on the Fife Arms Hotel at Braemar, where the enterprising owner was determined to match any Alpine resort. Great preparations had been made for winter sports: bridges were thrown over the larger burns; arrangements were made for hot coffee to be served at many cottages; wire was lifted to form nursery slopes; curling and skating parks were cleaned out and huts erected at each one. A toboggan run was prepared and, for the first time in Scotland, a Swiss instructor was engaged to give ski lessons. The Ski Club of Great Britain was

44

officially represented and from London came a first class band. The hotel was packed and even sitting rooms had to be used as bedrooms. Unfortunately, the thin mantle of snow that greeted guests on their arrival had disappeared by next morning, and no more snow fell until the middle of March. It was the most snowless winter in Scotland this century, a bizarre situation as there had been a heavy fall in Barcelona on February 11th and on the same day, the port of Dover was closed for 24 hours, owing to a tremendous blizzard in the Channel.

Membership of the Scottish Ski Club nevertheless continued to rise. In spite of the lack of snow more and more Scots found out that there was fun to be had among the Scottish hills in winter, as the tone of this jingle implies:

> "Ah stertit tae ski
> But Ah crashed oan ma bunnet,
> Ower near tae yon scree
> Ah stertit tae ski
> And tak it frae me
> That Ah shouldna hae dun it,
> Ah stertit tae ski
> But Ah crashed oan ma bunnet."

It was possible now to have a week's holiday in winter at Fortingal Hotel for four guineas. Lawers Hotel at Kenmore was three guineas, Blair Atholl, five, but Simpson's Temperance in Newtonmore, only two. A week at the four star Fife Arms, Braemar, five guineas, dinner in Fort William at the Station Hotel cost 2/6d. Alternatively one could have seventeen days in Norway for £15 1s. This included first class steamer, railway, good hotel, plus full board.

Harold Mitchell felt that racing could thrive in Scotland, as often a sheltered gully would hold enough snow for a competition, while overall conditions ruled out "a good day on the tops". He was a great believer in tests for improving standards of skiing. He himself learned to ski by trial, "fall would be a better word" and error. He did not begin skiing until he left Oxford and then immediately attempted to pass the third class test of the Ski Club of Great Britain. "With some twenty other aspirants, I climbed in deep powder snow through a wooded hillside in the Engadine. I was young, fit and knew only one turn – a telemark to the left. We simply had to get down within a certain time, but alas, I telemarked into a tree and failed ignominiously." Having mastered a turn in the other direction, he then entered any competition that was available, winning his first proper race, the Lauberhorn Cup, at Wengen, in 1924.

46

At the annual dinner of the Scottish Ski Club in November, 1933, Harold Mitchell invited his friend Arnold Lunn to address the club on the question of competitive skiing. Lunn, a humorous speaker, flattered the club by saying that ski racing owed a tremendous debt to Scottish representatives. So stimulated, the Scottish Ski Club resolved to hold a race as soon as snow conditions were right. This led to the following report in the Club Journal: "February, 1934, was as warm and dry as many a Scottish summer and members indulged in premature clout-casting were probably surprised to receive a circular from the committee, intimating that the first slalom race to be organised by the club would take place during the first weekend in March. As a matter of fact, this was the only date suitable to Harold Mitchell, and he had to be there because the race committee needed his experience. A fall of snow late in February sent hopes of carrying the programme through on the chosen date, soaring, only to droop quickly with a subsequent storm. Reports of snow were conflicting and vague, so two representatives motored up on 27th February to make a personal examination of the terrain. A few streaky white patches on the highest peaks constituted the only snow, so it was obviously ridiculous to think of holding the race. In spite of frequent observations taken through the bar window of the hotel, there was no appreciable improvement, and it only remained to distribute the bad news among the members.

Snow fell some days later, and it was hastily decided to hold the races on 10th and 11th March. Two members impressively arrayed with stop watches, the S.C.G.B. official handbook, plenty of pencils and notebooks, went up to Killin on Friday evening, ostensibly to make such preparations for the dinner as were necessary, but really to see that there was no funny business about their bedrooms, and baths etc. They optimistically tried to book rooms for various people, who had casually asked them to do so, and spent an entertaining half hour with a very efficient lady in the office trying to fit nine assorted husbands and wives, bachelors and spinsters, into two staff rooms and an attic.

Harry MacRobert, who happened also to be in the hotel, was co-opted by the committee, and made to help in writing out the names of probable starters, and in mastering the rules with regard to what part of the person had to pass through the flags to avoid disqualification. At intervals through the evening, telephone calls from newspapers came in, making sundry inquiries. The society editor of the *Scotsman* wanted to know if any people with titles would be there, and if so, whom? They were regretfully told that we could not say. 'Well, any well-known Edinburgh people?' The writer's name did not seem to mean much to him, and he rather disappointedly rang off. The *Glasgow Herald* did not

ring up until after the race, and then they rang to see where the photographer should stand in order to take the best photographs.

The weather next day was not very good; still it wasn't raining and it wasn't thawing. A depressed salmon fisher who had been driven off the loch by the high wind, made us anticipate a good blow on the hill. Lady Raeburn, who had undertaken to set the course, arrived commendably early and we proceeded to the hut where conditions were as bad as we expected – high wind, driving snow and very cold.

Not long after the official hour for the kick-off, the names of all entrants were put into a hat and solemnly drawn for the order of starting. The whole party, competitors, photographers, spectators, officials, and a few interested dogs, then moved off in an imposing cavalcade to a moderately steep bit of the hill on the west side of the valley which leads up to the Beinn Ghlas hut where the course was chosen and the flags stuck in. There then appeared several small groups of intending competitors, gradually recovering from a ball which they had attended and now progressing painfully towards the venue. They wished to compete, and their names had not been included in the draw. A further draw in that biting wind was unthinkable, so the names were added to the list in order of their arrival.

The first slalom race ever held in Britain then started. The snow, after being broken up and stamped down was perfectly good, rather slow and quite easy. Just how easy, was soon shown by Patricia Raeburn, who made a flawless descent. The majority of competitors found a certain amount of trouble in negotiating the course, but it was not sufficiently difficult to distinguish properly the good runners from the moderate competitors. For the second run, conditions which had been tolerable became really bad and the intense cold was supplemented by snow falling as well as being blown across the hill, which rendered visibility very poor and was a severe handicap to those who were in the last places. The show was carried through somehow then everyone scrambled back to the hotel to the comforts of drinks, fires and baths. High praise is due to the fortitude of those who acted as time keepers and starters in the ghastly weather, and the perfect legible record of the times was duly carried back to the hotel where the results were worked out. The flag keeping was disgraceful and for this, the committee, rather than the flagkeepers, must take the blame, but although some people got away with some glaring faults, it did not affect the placing of those two runners who were comfortably ahead of the rest, and who made no errors. A dinner was held in the Killin Hotel in the evening and was attended by nearly sixty people. It was in the course of this meal that the committee woke up to the fact that they had forgotten to arrange for a cup, which it was

Opposite. The first slalom race to be held in Scotland, March 10th 1934. Lady Raeburn on left. Her daughter, the winner, in the foreground. Harry MacRobert fourth from the left. (MacRobert Album)

The Pitman Quaich, donated to the Scottish Ski Club in 1934. This cup is still presented each year.

anticipated was to be awarded to the winner. They had meant to approach Mr. J.S. Pitman (who, it was rumoured had already indicated to his son that he was thinking of giving a cup) with tact, and charm, but there was now no time for finesse. The following telegram was drafted out and flushed with wine, the assembled company roared approval of its dispatch. 'Fifty five members of the Scottish Ski Club present their compliments to their oldest member and intimate that Miss Patricia Raeburn has won the first open slalom race held in Scotland. At present, no cup.' From Mr. Pitman, a telegram was received next morning, and it appeared that he was not irritated by this brutal attack, for he said – 'Delighted to give cup for race' and the Pitman Quaich which will be competed for annually, is the happy result."

KILLIN SLALOM RACE 1934

1.	Miss P. Raeburn	20.6	28	48.6
2.	A.F. Wallace	26.4	22.8	49.2
3.	W.R. Higginbotham	25	31.9	56.9

The race generated an extraordinary amount of enthusiasm and fun, although the weather had been appalling. This was typical of Scottish skiing, then and now, and points to the significant difference between people who ski happily in Scotland and those to be found in the Alps. Scottish skiers have an unlimited capacity to put their head down against a blizzard, knowing that eventually the sun will shine and conditions equal those on the continent. At heart, all Scottish skiers have to be mountaineers, that is, people who love the hills in all weathers and have mastered the ability to travel in them in all conditions.

Opposite. Neil MacKenzie, fifth in the Pitman Quaich, 1935. (L.J. Macrae)

The Scottish weekenders now realised that the adrenalin of competition gave an extra dimension to their skiing. The Pitman Quaich had been a success. However, it did not offer much fun to the poor skier. In order to give all competitors an equal chance, another member of the club, Norman Hird, presented a trophy for a handicap slalom. The race committee now had to tackle the difficult business of handicapping entrants whose abilities varied from almost total incapacity to turn at all, to those who had experience in slalom racing abroad. Many competitors could not give the committee any idea of their ability, particularly if they were of the "old school tie brigade" who believed in exaggerated attempts at false modesty. Handicaps were to be deducted at the start, so theoretically, everyone should pass the winning post together. Entrants were divided into six classes. Each then lined up in a row, the largest handicaps actually on the starting line, with the class behind ready to step forward as the one ahead moved off. At the word "go", the ultra-rabbits went off, ten seconds later, the rabbits, followed by the sheep,

Opposite. The finishing line of the first Hird Trophy race, 8th March 1936. Robertson in front. (H. MacRobert Album)

then the goats, infra-tigers, and finally, the tigers. "It is not meant to be a slalom" someone said, "but dodging through the corpses will make it something jolly like one." The Hird Trophy race became one of many held regularly near the Beinn Ghlas hut. Ronald Higginbotham was usually the starter. He also chose the course, which ran from a big rock on the Corronaich side of the col. Higginbotham stood on this rock for the duration of the race and soon it was known by his name.

With the introduction of races, the standard of skiing began to rise. In 1936, heavy snow fell in November, and hundreds of people were to be seen skiing in and around Edinburgh and Glasgow. By December, so many people were skiing in the Lawers district that a notice appeared in the press urging them to ski elsewhere, due to the congestion, not only on the mountains, but also on the road, which was quite inadequate for the traffic it had to bear at weekends. Many people now had cars and this led to a complaint in the press that: "it seems that the drivers fell into two camps. Either skidaddlers or skidawdlers, the former are those whose vehicle skedaddles all over the road,and so has to be pushed, and the latter are those who do the pushing. It is claimed that non-skiers come to watch the sport and have been amazed at the alacrity with which a skier will jump from his comfortable car into a blizzard, in order to assist on his way, one less fortunate than himself. However, this is not due to decency or sportsmanship but purely to the plain fact that one of those fools has gone and blocked the road again and until he is pushed out of the way, no-one can get up."

Another problem facing the driver was that of transporting his skis. Inventions were many, the criterion being that the apparatus "should disfigure the car as little as possible so that its second hand value would be maintained, and it will not depreciate because of a large hole in the roof, where once your skis used to raise their points to Heaven."

The senior racing club on the continent, the Kandahar, presented a cup to the Scottish Ski Club, to be competed for in an "open straight race" in Scotland. It had been considered that a straight race was far too dangerous to encourage officially, but now that the standard of skiing had improved, and skiers' "boldness and dash increased", it was decided to try. The course was to start from the summit of Beinn Ghlas, and after crossing the almost level plateau, competitors had to run down the east side of the gully, which cut deeply into the south face of the hill. In all, the descent was about 1,250 feet. The official report of this race which was sent to the editor of the Scottish Ski Club journal, enclosed the following letter: "I enclose herewith the official report of the Scottish Kandahar race, for which you asked, but it is impersonal, and does not give you any idea of the absolute horror with which I, and no doubt,

Opposite. Crowds gathering at the Scottish Ski Club hut, Beinn Ghlas, on the day of the Hird Trophy race, 1936. (H. MacRobert Album)

The Citroen Kegresse shooting brake, loaned to the Scottish Ski Club, on the hills above Killin, 1937. (Scottish Ski Club Journal)

many of the other competitors, viewed the little string of flags which marked the course down, what is, to all intents and purposes, a precipice! I have often been on Beinn Ghlas, and have even occasionally, looked down this south gully but have always recoiled from the edge of it with a feeling of sick horror, and certainly, the idea of racing down in a mist had never occurred to me, even in my wildest nightmares. I think it remarkable that seventeen people should have been brave enough to face the starter, although it is possible that this number would have been reduced if the course setter had not the devilish cunning to arrange that the start should be from the very summit of Beinn Ghlas, so that anyone trying to back out at the last moment, found himself backing down the north cliffs of the mountain. Some people seem to think that the event should have been declared 'no race' on account of the mist, which certainly got much worse as the race progressed, but I think that in view of the careful way in which the course had been flagged, there was no necessity." The race was won by D.G. Drakeford, in one minute, six seconds. He had already won the Pitman Quaich and now held the first Harold Mitchell Scottish Championship cup.

As a foreign visitor remarked at the time, "Skiers in Scotland are afraid of nothing. I have seen them ski down slopes which elsewhere would have been recognised as meadow, but no, here it is considered an excellent skiing slope, just as long as there is a little snow buried between the grass. Adaptability and agility are truly great virtues of skiing, and that is where the skiers of Scotland excel." The writer pled for a large scale map of the more popular skiing districts, as he complained, "I have wandered about many a time in thick fog, for valuable hours, looking for a hut, let alone the snow."

Wandering through the fog, this foreigner might have come across a large, grey, unwieldy looking vehicle, in the neighbourhood of Killin. This was the Citroen Kegresse shooting brake, which Mr. Andrew Reid of Auchterarder had lent the Scottish Ski Club for experimental purposes. With the emergence of uplift in the Alps, the club committee had been plagued with suggestions, some more ludicrous than others, but all patently impracticable, for transporting members uphill without the expenditure of physical effort. The shooting brake was therefore trundled up towards the hut, but the conclusion was that it was not a success. "The ski club secretary is particularly gratified by the committee's decision as he found that he was not really popular when endeavouring to collect tractor fares which were almost unanimously described as exorbitant. He has, however, now developed such a fellow feeling for bus and tram car conductors that it is almost impossible for him to board a car without enquiring how the takings were working out."

Meanwhile enthusiasts from Dundee were skiing in the area around the Cairnwell, meeting each other over coffee and sandwiches as they sheltered from the wind in the lee of large snowdrifts. The outcome was the formation of the Dundee Ski Club, on the 1st December 1936. The difficulty with their area was that the club depended on the Glenshee road being open, otherwise it was impossible for skiers to reach the hills. A survey of snow cover was gleaned from Glenshee inhabitants, and it was realised that snow lay from early January until late April in the gully of Glas Maol about a mile to the east of the summit of the Cairnwell. This was mapped out on a large scale plan which was hung in the Spittal Hotel. The club overflowed from this hotel and so rented a cottage in Glenshee. Members staying here had a bonus in early 1939, when the Braemar road was specially opened to permit the passage of a funeral, allowing skiers to reach the summit of the road in deep perfect snow for the first time.

As the winter progressed, skiers returning from the Alps were remarking that "Heil Hitler" had been substituted for "gruss gott" as a salutation. By the end of the year, almost all of the men belonging to the Dundee Ski Club were on active service, and any members of the Scottish Ski Club on the hills were in uniform. One of the first to be killed was the Scottish champion, Dudley Drakeford.

At the end of the road, Achlean, Glen Feshie, during the New Year meet of the Scottish Ski Club, 1939. (MacRobert Album)

4. WAR INTERLUDE

Opposite. Norwegian soldiers, their skis were made in Dumfries out of Scots Pine from Glenmore Forest. (Norwegian Government archives)

Opposite. Near Forest Lodge, Abernethy 1943. On the right General Sir Colin Gubbins, C.O. of the Special Operations Executive, to his right is the Norwegian expert on "Heavy Water", Professor Major Leif Tronstad. (Norwegian Government archives)

Norwegian troops on exercise, they were based in Rothiemurchus, where they trained for the attack on the "Heavy Water" installation in Norway.
(Norwegian Government archives)

At the start of the war, it was assumed that the main confrontation between the allies and the Germans would be on the Norwegian front. The British, unlike the Germans with their crack mountain division, the Gebirgsjager, had however no units specially trained in mountain warfare. To remedy the situation, Colonel Andrew Croft was appointed officer in charge of arctic warfare, and asked to start a school in Scotland to train troops in winter conditions. He was joined by Captain Martin Lindsay who had had considerable experience of the Arctic and only a few years before had lead the British Trans-Greenland Expedition on a record unsupported dog-sledge journey of 1,050 miles.

Troops were stationed throughout the Highlands. The 52nd Lowland Division was in Cluny, the 6th Cameronians in Glen Feshie and the 7th/9th Royal Scots at Derry Lodge. With the occupation of Norway a steady stream of Norwegians arrived in Scotland via Shetland. They were formed into the Norwegian Brigade and were based in Abernethy. The Norwegian Commando Unit, Kompani Linge, had the use of Drumintoul Lodge in Rothiemurchus. The skis that were needed for their training were made in Dumfries out of Scots Pine from Glenmore Forest.

Forest Lodge, in Abernethy, had been commandeered for British troops. Brigadier John Hunt and Frank Smythe of Everest fame, were stationed there with orders to train the men to ski. Hunt remembered recently that: "It proved a novel experience of not unmixed pleasure. A great expanse of heather, not much snow, stupendous loads and fierce Cairngorm blizzards. On one occasion fighting the way up to Loch Etchachan, in the teeth of a gale, I watched Smythe lifted by some gust and deposited forty feet below the track in a snow drift. But the troops enjoyed it and we gained much experience of the conditions of winter warfare which was to be useful later on, even though the troops we trained were committed on the coasts of Europe."

The junior staff for the schools of mountain warfare set up in the various lodges on the fringe of the Cairngorms were selected in a haphazard fashion. As Frank Sutton recollected: "For me, the whole thing started, when, in 1942, one of the circulars which officers had to read asked for the names of those with skiing experience, so I put my name down. The following January, I was sent a temporary posting to 156 Brigade, winter training school, 52nd Division at Glen Cluny Lodge. When I reported to the acting adjutant, I was told that I was a ski instructor. The chief, a captain, collected about a dozen of us, mostly lieutenants like myself, but also some sergeants, and in a few days we went through the whole syllabus. There was very little snow and what there was lay on north and east facing slopes towards Macdhui. The men made good progress. They were mostly tough miners from Lanarkshire who had never been in the mountains before. When I had my first squad lined up on the top of a small, gentle slope, I thought I would make myself popular and said 'There is nothing in it boys, just push off, close your eyes and wait for the crash.' Which I did, but opened my eyes, when I stopped with a snow plough, but they did not! The result was a bit of a shambles, so I never said that again."

The emphasis was on drill before learning to ski. The following is a typical example of the first day's instruction:

"*52nd Division Ski Drill*

1. Names of ski parts. Ski, tip, turn up, heel, sole, top, toe iron, foot plate, toe strap, heelspring, lever.
2. Method of binding skis together. Sole to sole, with strap or cord at heel and turn up. If only one strap or cord is available, it is put in centre.
3. Position of 'At Ease'. Feet 30" apart, skis together in left hand close to side, hand grasping the skis above the bindings, (approx. chest high). Sticks together in right hand close to body, hand grasping the sticks at the top (approx. chest high).
4. Position of 'Attention'. As for the position of 'At Ease' except that the feet are in the normal position of 'Attention'.
5. Carry position. The word of command 'Carry Sticks' is given when facing a flank.
   (i) Turn right hand over and grasp sticks about 1 ft. from the top. Swing the sticks over right shoulder, baskets to the rear.
   (ii) Slide hand down skis towards the heel, leaning skis towards the shoulder bending down as far as possible so that the bindings are on the shoulders.
   (iii) Raise body, at the same time, slipping skis up so that bindings are behind shoulder.
   Slip left hand down to heel, grasping skis as for butt of rifle.

From this position, the squads can be marched off with the skis resting on the sticks.

6. 'For inspection show skis'. Stick ski sticks in the snow. Turn the soles of both skis to the front, one in each hand.

7. 'Order skis'. Reverse of the 'Carry'.

8. 'Ground skis'. Skis are laid on the ground on the left side of the man, tips to the front: sticks on the right, baskets to the rear."

Mountains, and arctic conditions were a completely new experience for most of the men. Martin Lindsay tried to teach them that the new environment was not necessarily hostile. He composed a lecture on the "friendly Arctic" to encourage a more sympathetic attitude to life and travel in a mountainous region.

The 52nd Lowland Division spent the best part of three years in the area bounded by the rivers Don, Dee, Spey and Findhorn. Soldiers bridged rivers, straightened roads and brought into the region variety and even prosperity. Troops were everywhere. Some local inhabitants were once startled to meet dark men in khaki turbans leading horses and mules along the paths beside the Spey. These were the Gurkhas brought into the district to maintain the supplies with troops camping higher up in the snow.

Pre-war uniform was completely inadequate for mountain conditions, wet trousers became sheets of ice hindering movement and army issue boots useless on wind polished snow. Problems of keeping warm had to be solved. As the months of mountain training went by it was discovered that a string vest was a great improvement on an ordinary woollen one. The army invented long johns and found out that they had to be seamless otherwise they caused ankle sores in wet snow.

The padre of the 52nd Division was the Reverend J.S. Wood. He recollected that in spite of the poor equipment the Jocks enjoyed their stay in the mountains. They were keen to learn to ski, making jumps before they could even go straight, with the Glasgow keelies the most enthusiastic. Occasionally the men suffered from loneliness and when living in snow holes would dig a network of tunnels in order to visit each other. The Jocks also became adept at supplementing the army rations with venison.

As mountain training proceeded, it became obvious that rapid transport for men and weapons over rough ground was a major problem. Sledges, wheels and jeeps had limitations for any large scale movement over the snow. The Americans had been working on a new type of vehicle using British specifications. It was a tracked vehicle that imposed on the surface a pressure of only one pound per inch as compared with

Standard issue uniform was inadequate
for mountain conditions. No 3
Commando training near Killin 1942.
(Imperial War Museum)

Jumping before they could walk; No 3
Commando training near Killin, 1942.
(Imperial War Museum)

Many good days skiing were enjoyed during the war. On the way to Cairngorm, March 1941. (W. Spiers)

Opposite. Late spring snow lying in the Einich Coire, Braeriach, enjoyed during a leave spent in the hills, 1942. (Dick West)

the four and a half pounds of a normal soldier or thirty pounds of a loaded mule. This meant that instead of sinking in, the vehicle could travel over deep snow or soft bog. It could even sail in reasonably calm waters. The new vehicle known as the "weasel" was brought back to Britain by men of the 52nd. All experimental work on it was carried out in the Cairngorms.

It seems, from the memoirs of wartime generals, that one of the aims of the retention of the 52nd Division in Scotland along with a detachment of the Norwegian Brigade, was to persuade German intelligence that an invasion of Scandinavia was planned. As it happened the mountain training was never put to the test. After a gruelling course in mountain warfare, a lieutenant wrote in his diary: "Then, at last, in October, we went by train to Southampton, crossed the channel by sea, landed in Ostende. A few days later we went into action — below sea level."

The training nevertheless had its long term benefits, as large numbers of men were introduced to the excitement and pleasure to be had from the Scottish hills in winter particularly if they could ski. One member of the Scottish Ski Club who managed to use his skis during the war was M.C. McKenzie. He remembered a trip North in 1944: "Within a week or two, came the first great snow of the war. On the Kilpatrick Hills, it fell colder and drier than ever remembered in Scotland. The first fall, nearly two feet of the lightest powder, was easily cleared off the roads, and then, by hanging on to thirty foot ropes, tied to cars driven furiously down the swept road, one was able to 'skijore' through the dry powder lying on the bumpy fields, with enormous exhilaration, and the certainty that F.I.S. times were being easily surpassed. As one became airborne after each bump, the sport was unusually thrilling and the car drivers only slightly spoilt it with their sadly unimaginative speedometer readings. After several further heavy snow falls, appeals were made to succour marooned A.A. units. These, it was stated, would have to abandon their posts or starve, unless food reached them by ski. Several relief expeditions were quickly organised by the club. Unfortunately, a man in a rather cold hut, feeding bits of icy peat into an ill-tempered stove and cut off from civilisation, in the snowy wastes, does not regard an enormous sack of potatoes, langlaufed six miles to his door, as a princely gift. 'Gawd, spuds again. Ain't they ever sending us meat and fags?' was about the best one could expect, and got."

The Cairngorms provided excellent spring snow for more than two months, and it was estimated that the corries held up to fifteen feet of snow by the beginning of March, and the Glen Einich schuss still afforded 1,600 feet of continuous running by the middle of May. In April

of the same year, another ski club member snatched five days leave in Aviemore. He remembered stepping off the London train into a little Austin taxi in its 200,000th mile. It took him up to Glenmore Lodge, each day. The spring snow lay in patches as low as the forest path and the main corrie was full all the way down to the river, a continuous run of over two miles. "Scottish sun shone proudly forth and on the climb up through the forest, all possible clothes were discarded."

M. C. McKenzie returned to Scotland in March 1944 when: "Dalwhinnie looked for all the world like a Tyrol village. Here the roads swarmed with bronzed soldiers and skis were everywhere. They had skied every day except two since Christmas, and for the five days that we were there, although cloud lay on the tops, the snow itself was good. Transport to the mountains was by autocycle, towing a bicycle, skis and sticks being clutched with one hand, and the handle bars with the other. Now, an autocycle has its clutch and throttle on different handle bars and a towed push bike, moving or stationary, is an unruly thing on snow, if you were bouncing skis and sticks in the wind. An admiring crowd, full of witty cracks and unhelpful advice, gathered each morning to watch the start."

On one occasion, McKenzie passed some Norwegian soldiers at Glenmore Lodge, "lying skuddy" in the sun, grateful apparently for having the day off from skiing. They had been living in snow holes and when asked what kind of night they had had, they replied that although they could not recommend it, a snow hole was undoubtedly the cheapest form of Scottish holiday.

Dick West managed to ski quite regularly during the war years. He and a party of friends from Glasgow would take the train to Newtonmore, where they would be met by a pretty girl and several horses. These belonged to the Norwegian army but the girl had an appropriate boyfriend and so was able to have the use of the horses to help Dick West and his friends reach the snow. Sometimes, they would take bicycles instead, stowing them away in the guard's van at the start of the journey then alighting late at night, usually in a blizzard, being faced with the prospect of attaching the skis to the bike.

Another wartime skier was W.B. Spiers. As he had organised the last pre-war meet of the Scottish Ski Club at Glenmore Lodge, he knew who to contact for permission to use the Lodge again. He longed to ski in the Cairngorms but having no petrol, looked for a friend who had access to the precious fuel. He found one, the duty officer with the bomb disposal unit for Clydeside. Settled weather greeted them after a long drive and at last they bumped over the rough track towards the Lodge. They were surprised to see lights, and when they arrived, they found that a small group of soldiers was already established. Spiers's friend, owing to his position with the bomb disposal unit, was wearing his navy-type hat. This led the officer in charge to remark that he had not been informed that the navy was coming to share their accommodation. Spiers was frightened to admit that in fact this was not an official party in case they were evicted. Instead, they carried out the subterfuge for the entire weekend, making full use of the military transport, right up to the snow line each day. On the second day, a message had arrived at the Lodge, calling Spiers's companion back to duty in Glasgow. It was a magnificent day, the sun sparkling on the snow and the two men could not resist turning a blind eye, knowing that they would be returning anyway later in the evening. When they eventually arrived back on the Clyde, they found that the entire workforce of John Brown's shipyard had been evacuated, owing to a land mine being suspended in a rafter.

To many soldiers the Scottish hills meant excitement and escape from the dreariness of barrack room life south of the border:

Eight Day Leave
The sights, the sounds, the smells of war,
The barrack room, the old mess hall,
We're so sick of that, you wouldn't believe
So we're off to the north on an eight day leave.

Our skis have no wax and there's moths in our socks,
But the mountains are there and there's snow on the tops,
Ben Lawers, Cairngorm, Braeriach, Beinn Ghlas,
And weather's all right, but look out for the grass.

We've climbed to the top, about 4,000 feet,
With a gale in our teeth and occasional sleet
But our spirits are high and we throw away care,
In that hissing schuss down with the wind in our hair.

Oh, it's always rewarding, a glorious scene,
With the mountains forever patient, serene,
And the loch and the air and the ptarmigan call,
When we're back at our toil, we remember it all.

So we pack up our ski and our uniforms don,
Have a drink with our friends, God! that train will have gone,
With knots straightened out we go back to our parts,
We return to the war, but there's peace in our hearts.

5. UPLIFT

Masses of enthusiastic skiers returned home in 1945. The wartime training of mountain troops and numerous leaves in Alpine centres had produced a large number of people determined to continue to ski. Foreign currency was short and skiers were left with little alternative but Scotland. The president of the Scottish Ski Club, Sir Harold Mitchell was determined that the club should adapt to the new circumstances and invited members to a cocktail party at his house. When they arrived he announced that the gathering was really an official general meeting of the club. The pre-war secretary, Higginbotham, pointed out that the popularity of skiing in Scotland was definitely established and he urged the committee to waive the touring qualifications of admission so that the large number of ex-army skiers could join at once.

With the rules altered, the Scottish Ski Club expanded quickly. The hut on Beinn Ghlas, was refurbished, two lavatories and an incinerator were added and Calor gas was installed. A notice was hung on the door. It read "Be warned of the smell of garlic — it's not last week's sandwiches but gas in the most explosive state."

Most skiers had now experienced the benefits of lift systems in the Alps, and urged their committee to provide some similar facility in Scotland. After much discussion it was decided that a weasel could answer this need. This was the vehicle with wide tracks used in snow, developed by 52nd Lowland Division during the war. It was reported that a weasel could not only make light work of the climb to the club hut but it would even be able to reach the summit of the mountain. There was also much discussion as to a bigger and better club hut. A stone building was suggested with a fireplace and bunks to sleep in overnight. The idea was put across that it should be built by the members themselves and the obvious material suggested was to be acquired by blowing up Higginbotham's rock and replacing that landmark by a stone hut. It was mooted that perhaps the junior members could be induced to cut peat during summer weekends as it was certainly abundant in the vicinity of the present hut.

People were now skiing in Scotland who would not have considered doing so before the war. They were warned by Dick West, an inveterate enthusiast, that: "The weather is always indifferent to bad, and the great mistake lies in waiting for a good day, as it seldom happens. Acquire a waterproof kit, and don't pay any attention to the prospect of rain. It is a curious fact that spring snow which provides 90% of the skiing in Scotland, is made faster by heavy rain. Great enjoyment is always available once the art of indifference to the weather has been mastered. The greatest handicap is suffered by those who cannot do without their spectacles and for them the use of the new-fangled contact lens, will come as a boon. The wind is a greater trial than the rain, and cannot be surmounted without strength. For this reason, women can seldom get as much fun out of Scotland on the snow. It is essential to get legs and lungs into good shape, so that one can be on the move all day. Never sit down. Sandwiches must be eaten while walking up and sweeties may be sucked on the way down. A header sometimes spirits the sweety away, but it tastes even better if the owner should chance to retrieve it from its snowy grave."

Dick West added that in Scotland the best snow lay in patches, in horizontal banks, or else in deep, and often narrow gullies. These corries and burn courses were skiing highways in the surrounding heather and even in mist provided excellent fun. He cautioned them however, that the first ascent should be made with care, in case the snow was weak. He added that if they could hear the sound of running water it meant that the continuous bridge over the stream was most likely to break through in the middle.

Equipment was now readily available. American ex-army skis, painted white, with protruding steel edges, cost £5. An enterprising Glasgow member of the club had bought up a large quantity of used Swiss Army equipment, and these skis plus white bamboo sticks, cost £3.10s. a pair. Skiers of all shapes and sizes and ages were clad from top to bottom in camouflage clothing, bought for a few shillings from the ex-W.D. shops that were springing up in all the cities.

The cars that had given skiers mobility in the thirties were now useless. Petrol rationing meant that the only means of transport to the snow was by bus. The Scottish Ski Club had been divided into sections and each now organised "Winter Sports Specials" that set off on early Sunday morning and picked up skiers en route. These buses threw people together and were a boost to club membership. One Scottish Ski Club member reported that: "Once you got over being a bit toffy-nosed about buses in general the thirty-two seater provided quite a comfortable mobile ski hut cum-changing room, gossip room, bar and buffet. Our bus departed from the George Hotel, Perth, at 10.15, and with the door-to-door collection, there was a lot to be said for it, particularly, the wonderful sense of ease and comfort the bus spirit, and maybe the other spirit, gave to one as we ended our irresponsible way homewards."

Early in the winter of 1946/47 there was a phenomenal fall of snow. So much so that roads were completely blocked, particularly round the Stirling area. Earl MacEwan, a member of the Scottish Ski Club, was the son of the owner of a large grocer's shop patronised by the surrounding farmers, who were unable to come to town to pick up their stores. The Stirling section of the Scottish Ski Club came to their rescue. Under the organisation of Earl they packed rucksacks with groceries and skied to the farms. They were not always received with enthusiasm however. One skier remembers arriving exhausted at a farm longing for a cup of tea. As he handed over the rucksack to a red faced woman she felt the weight and remarked, "Rice and flour, why didn't you bring us some chocolate biscuits?"

The unexpected snow had also cut off the Noranside Sanatorium near Dundee. On the first Friday night of the snow fall, the leader of the Tannadice Scouts, Major C.F.I. Neish, learned that a hundred and fifty loaves of bread were lying at a point some four and a half miles from the sanatorium, and that neither tractors nor sledges could get through. He immediately volunteered to deliver the supplies with his scouts, whom he had already trained to ski.

The scouts set out in the morning for the sanatorium. The first two miles were hard work as they did not own skis. The strong east wind was whipping up the dry snow on the fields forming blinding sheets and they had to negotiate drifts of up to fifteen feet in depth. Landmarks had vanished, one cottage was completely submerged, and often it was difficult for the boys to tell the direction of the road. They lunched in the lee of an abandoned car and eventually reached the sanatorium.

As the prolonged snowstorms of 1947 built up, the scouts became the "voyageurs" of the district, running meat, mail and even urgent supplies of baby food into isolated areas. They were once called upon to put the local police force on skis to enable them to carry out urgent duties. Out of this experience, the scouts set up a regular ski service. During the same snow fall, three hydro board linesmen were feared lost on the Lecht road near Tomintoul. After 24 hours silence Brigadier Sir John Forbes, set out to search. He skied for 14 miles up the road above Cockbridge and eventually came across the men at 2,000 feet, in a 20 foot drift.

The first peace time ski school in Scotland was set up in the early winter of 1948 by Captain Bill Bracken. A renowned pre-war racer, he had learnt to ski in Austria where his father owned a chalet, and had won

Easter meets of the Scottish Ski Club
were centered at the Aviemore Hotel,
since burnt to the ground and replaced
by the Strathspey Hotel.
(P.N. Rankin)

Bill Bracken, centre, a former captain of
the British Ski team, ran a ski school in
Drumochter in the winter of 1948/49.
(Dick West)

all the classic British Alpine races, many of them several times. Captain of the British Team in 1929, he was well known by Alpine skiers for his enthusiasm and for the immaculate style of his skiing. He was said, by Arnold Lunn, to have been the first to perfect the parallel turn. His racing days over, he had opened a ski school in Zermatt in 1936, which he ran until the war. His pupils had mostly been English holidaymakers, army officers and public school boys, and included the current world champion. During the war Captain Bracken had been posted to Pitmain Lodge near Kingussie as an instructor to the Lowland Division. Now that the Government had withdrawn all foreign currency allowances, none of Bracken's clients could reach his school in Zermatt. He decided therefore to set it up in Scotland instead. Remembering his days near Dalwhinnie he decided that the area near Drumochter would make an ideal site, as it was close to the railway.

A cartoonist for Punch, David Langdon, was one of Captain Bracken's first clients. The magazine immediately christened it the "MacMurren School" and this publicity brought fame and pupils to the small patch of snow at the back of Drumochter Lodge. Bracken worked in conjunction with Lesley Ling, who ran a bus service from the Midlands as well as organising a cheap fare on the railway. If clients had come by train, they were met at 4 a.m. on the platform and transported to the lodge nearby, where Mrs Babs Bracken was hostess, chaperone, guide and part time bar tender, helped by Captain Richardson, of Ski Club of Great Britain fame.

Skiing equipment, all ex-W.D., was provided for the pupils. One student of the Bracken School remembers that: "Waxing parade was made easy. The system was to carry your skis around the hotel after breakfast till you saw a back window emitting dense clouds of black smoke and coughing noises. Skis were then posted into the dim interior. After a gentle circuit via the bar, by following a smell of tarry ropes through the back premises, the professionally buttered article was collected from the other end of the system, except when the electric iron burned up the lighting flex, on which occasion it was very easy to hear all about skiing and other things besides.

The Brackennalp, was some way away, and a bus took us to Drumochter Lodge. Quite a short march took us to the nursery slope. The painful process that ensued is well known to all who ski. The staff divided to cope with the strivers and thrivers, and so we are brought from kindergarten to slalom, conducted running and racing always under a critical eye. Even the dimmest novice found he could enjoy some honest running after a short time."

The hills round Drumochter offered a great variety of runs. The top of what was called the Brackenalp could be reached in half an hour, giving two excellent circular routes back to the starting point – the perfect place for a ski school. The lower part of the alp contained an area where the snow spread out and was large enough to hold a sizeable class. Here Bill Bracken taught the beginners. As the season progressed, holes began to appear. Most pupils had no difficulty avoiding these, but one held a fascination for a Mrs. Attwood. She was at the "Stem turn" stage and inevitably, no matter from which side of the snow she started, she was drawn inexorably towards the hole. After five landings in it, like a golfball on the green, the hole was named "Mrs. Attwood's aperture". The ski school lasted three months and culminated with the holding of the MacMurren Derby, set on the Brackenalp on Easter Monday. The competitors, called "Francless Fanatics", came mostly from south of the border. The race was held on steep slopes above Drumochter with the path of the racecourse flagged all the way with gay notices reading "To the races". On nearing the slopes the competitors were further encouraged by the sound of the pipes floating down the wind and were finally greeted by the Bracken School's two dogs. One competitor remembered stopping here to watch Captain Richardson climbing up a semi-precipice to place 18 pairs of flags to ensure the unwary on the course. He had put down his sandwiches and now found to his fury that the Bracken dogs had gobbled them up, complete with rationed butter and black-market meat.

The finish of the race was clearly visible from the start. An official stood here with a huge flag, marking the end of the course so that there would be no confusion. Spectators were stationed at each pair of flags all the way down, and were to shout out to the next one every racer's time as declared by the starter. This was relayed to those at the finish and of course the racer himself. This method added to the interest and excitement to both spectators and competitors. At last everything was ready. Captain Bracken set off first at great speed and with perfect panache. At one point however, even with his newly sharpened steel edges he could not quite hold a turn on the fast spring snow. His time at the finish was 42 seconds. It was reported that a look of horror was seen to spread across the rugged features of the few Scottish Ski Club members who were competing and they were heard to mutter resolutions "to go canny". In the event, nearly all the Bracken School skiers came to grief, through being too impetuous, whereas the careful Scottish skiers took the first five places. One of the competitors, A.D. Butler, had broken both his legs in the Alps the previous January, while training for the Olympic Games, but he was said to have "completed

Opposite. Bill Bracken, centre with cap, musters his clients at Dalwhinnie Station.
(Dick West)

Opposite. Horses helped skiers reach the snow.
(Dick West)

one run down in excellent style. When fully recovered, he should go far in the racing world."

During the weekend, the weather had been fine, but as the last competitors came down the course a deluge of rain soaked everyone to the skin. Bill Bracken rose to the occasion, however, and supplied hot drinks in the bar of the Loch Ericht Hotel. By the next season, he had returned to Zermatt. "Just as well," remarked Earl MacEwan, "as no similar organisation could ever operate successfully in Scotland in a year when skiing in Switzerland was possible. Are people going to travel from, say London to Newtonmore, for some very spartan skiing, when it is permitted to spend £35 at Davos or Scheidegg?" Some Scots did manage to reach the Alps and returned with reports of a new attitude to the sport.

Instead of touring, skiers were converging on narrow glittering tracks termed "pistes" that wound down the hill, polished hard and smooth by the passage of hundreds of pairs of skis. On either side the snow was virgin. Down this track could be seen the new breed of skiers described as having: "Arms outstretched, travelling fast. A slight change of direction to avoid some excessive obstacle but mostly straight down, flat out and only when really necessary the new ski turn, the ruade, a forward leaning lounging check." The returning Scot explained that this new turn was possible with the bindings which now had more down-pull, and that also steel edges were built out from the sides of the ski in order to give a grip to the mirror-like surface of the piste. The pre-war skier was warned that his old-fashion parallel swing would only now produce a "soul shattering, bone shaking side slip". He now either had to change his style, or else ski very early in the morning after a fresh fall of snow before the piste had been made. This emphasis on downhill skiing had come about as a result of lifts that were springing up in all the Alpine resorts.

Scottish weekend skiers were now converging on two main areas, Killin, where activities centred round the Scottish Ski Club hut on Beinn Ghlas, and Glenshee. The Killin skiers were encouraged to hear of Hydro Board plans for a scheme at Lochan na Lairige. To carry out this work a road was to be built from Killin over the pass and down to the Bridge of Balgie. One skier remembers that they had visions of mountain boulevards and spacious car parks, ever snow-free. They imagined that they would be able to buy cheaply all the written-off lengths of railway line and assorted wire haulage gear which attended such schemes.

The land around the Lawers group of mountains had meanwhile been bought and then presented to the National Trust for Scotland by an anonymous donor. The Trust stated at the time that its purpose was to

Opposite. The Scottish Ski Club gathers in Glen Einich, 1947. (Murray Bell)

preserve these natural areas for the benefit and enjoyment of all, and such sports of climbing and skiing would be assured of receiving active support.

The Scottish Ski Club was particularly interested in the attitudes of the new landlord. Plans for erecting a permanent ski tow were now going ahead. Both the Dundee and the Scottish Ski Clubs had come to the conclusion at the same time that uplift was necessary for Scottish skiing to step into the new era. The first mention in the press of the Scottish Ski Club's involvement with a ski lift produced the following letter:

4th December 1947   Elmtree Road,
                                Lime,
                                Cheshire.

Have we sunk so low that we must carry the lazy city toilers up to the top and then launch them — vast crowds of them — down our treasured ski fields?

Is it wise to encourage such persons to venture into the vagaries of a Scottish winter, unable or unwilling to climb a couple of thousand feet? How will they react when exposed to a Highland blizzard whilst perched, unprotected on a crazy ski lift? What is likely to happen to them, standing chilled to the bone, soaked to the skin, whilst the ice cold mists shriek past at 80 m.p.h.? Will they have the stamina and perhaps the experience in dense cloud to slither down a piste which may be well nigh invisible? How many frost bitten fingers, noses, ears and even deaths from exposure are we going to have on our consciences?

Let them climb on their feet and thereby stimulate their circulation and increase powers of resistance to the elements. Ski lifts may be useful for fashionable crowds on the continent, where there are great areas and heights and not infrequently, warm sunshine and light breezes. Over here, our accessible ski areas are far more limited, our weather unpredictable, our accommodation sadly restricted.

Let us keep our Highland hills for those who find relaxation and joy in climbing them — whether in summer or winter, whether on foot or on ski, and beware of encouraging glorified tobogganing instead of real skiing.

Yours faithfully,
Theo Nicholson.

The Scottish Ski Club committee considered this letter and came to the conclusion that the diehard who protests against the introduction of ski lifts may do so for several reasons but that in their opinion, none of the arguments was valid. "He may merely disapprove of these new-fangled contraptions preferring a more spartan attitude to the sport. That is a perfectly reasonable opinion to which he is entitled but this does not give him the right to deny others the chance to take their sport as they like. He may argue that lifts will have a softening influence on the skiing population, and should be prohibited in their own interests but here the objector oversteps his rights by trying to interfere with the liberty of others. Perhaps the diehard feels on stronger ground when he sets himself up as a defender of the amenities of our Scottish mountains. This is more debatable, but there again, we would suggest he is wrong for the following reasons. There are so many mountains in Scotland, covering vast areas of desolation, and so little money with which to erect any forms of lifts, that there will always be a hundred virgin mountains for every one desecrated by a lift. As all the decadent skiers will be attracted as by a magnet to the lifts, the remaining slopes will be left in splendid isolation for the sole benefit of the diehards. With so much of our freedom snatched away, or sadly curtailed, Heaven forbid that we should not have freedom to build a lift if we can find the money and obtain permission from the landowner."

A syndicate of Scottish Ski Club members had now actually purchased a weasel and had had it running satisfactorily on their local grouse moor. However, they had to report to the club that "Unfortunately, the beast needs petrol, and so far this obstacle had not been overcome by the syndicate, which is a pity considering a weasel seems to be able to surmount anything."

The Dundee Ski Club, however with a membership of only 220, set the pace in improving facilities for skiers on the hills. On a wet Sunday, in July 1948, club members laid the foundations for two separate huts in Glenshee. The men working on the Ben Gulabin site had an easy job, but those on Glass Maol had a nightmare. The mist was down to 2,500 feet and the site at 3,000 feet just could not be found. A howling gale was blowing and rain lashing down as they struggled about laden with wooden runners, sledge hammers and spades in their search for the white painted marking pin that had been erected to identify the site. At last the pin was found, and the foundations laid.

Five months later at 6 a.m. a bus overflowing with club members left Dundee. They had come forward to help with the erection of the two huts. The summit of the road was reached at first light and in pouring rain the water-logged sections of the huts were picked up by the

Building the club hut in Glenshee.
(Dundee Ski Club Journal)

D. McBain with the innards of the
Glenshee Ski tow, 1954.
(Dundee Ski Club Journal)

Up by ropetow, Glenshee, 1952.
(Dundee Ski Club Journal)

occupants of the bus. As the light grew stronger, sections could be seen weaving their way up Glass Maol, looking like gigantic spiders with numerous legs. By 3.30 p.m. the job was complete, even to the finishing touches of provisioning the new huts with teapot, cups, primus and paraffin.

At the following A.G.M. the committee of the Dundee Ski Club was voted enough money for the construction of an experimental ski-tow. During the summer, an ex-army vehicle, fitted with a winch had been tried out on the Sidlaw Hills, working on an endless wire rope. The president of the ski club, Brigadier R.C. Hawman, was granted permission by the landlord of Glenshee, Farquharson of Invercauld, to erect a "contraption capable of being removed at short notice". This meant, of course, that the tow would have to be portable. However, with £150 in hand, the committee set about putting plans into effect. A two cylinder, air cooled 8 BHP 750 c.c. petrol engine was bought on December 2nd 1950 and despatched to Tom Ronald the chief engineer of the project. A fortnight later, the tow was working on Mount Blair in Glenshee, the first ski tow to be erected in Britain. A series of modifications followed as, in order to give the necessary reduction from an engine speed of 1,800 revs. per minute to 4 miles per hour on the endless rope, the driving pulleys had to be kept small, and to give the grip, they had to be increased to three with two jockeys. This was found to be too high a gear for using the pulleys as the capstan to pull the tow up the hill, but the fitting of a small gear box from a three-wheeler car gave the correct ratio. The whole apparatus was mounted on a wooden sledge fitted with well-lacquered ski-like runners. In this form, it ran very well for several months, by the end of which time, the rope began to object to the rough treatment of being buried by snow storms during the week, and then dug out at each weekend.

After splicing the rope several times, the tow was fitted with a two foot diameter driving pulley and rollers to guide the rope on and off, and re-erected on the Cairnwell. This was much more satisfactory, but now the machine had to run in bottom gear all the time in order to make up for the change of ratios. Not surprisingly, the gearbox stripped bottom gear and had to run in second, which made the art of attaching oneself to the rope extremely tricky, but this was compensated, according to a member of the club, "by the thrill of rushing uphill at 10 m.p.h."

At last though, with a grinding of teeth, the gearbox gave up the unequal struggle, and on 20th May, the tow was loaded on a lorry and sent back to the club's chief engineer. His plans for "ski tow, mark two" were luckily well advanced, and by the beginning of the second season, the new tow was in operation. Season tickets were available to members

79

at the cost of £1 a head. Day tickets were 2/6d. and strangers could become temporary members, for a further 2/6d. The moving rope was grasped by the hand, but the more enlightened members procured a "hookum". This was described as a "mousetrap cum tin opener device that had been devised by the citizens of Dundee when they found that their arms were becoming too long for their jackets."

At Killin, the Scottish Ski Club erected a Glenshee Mark 2 type of tow on the Beinn Ghlas col. It was placed there by the weasel which at last the club had managed to make mobile. Members could travel on this for 5/- from Bridge of Lochay right up to the hut. However, only the brave chanced the trip, because as Donnaie MacKenzie remembers: "With the advice of Ross MacLean, an eminent member of the Scottish bar 'conditions of travel' were printed on the tickets and signposts, under which passengers 'renounced to themselves and their heirs whomsoever all claims for death or other injury ...' There is also a condition that the club do not actually undertake to convey any passenger, whether he had paid or not, anywhere. That was just as well, because the weasel frequently did not make its destination. On one occasion, it went on fire and singed the President's pants. On another, there was deep, drifting snow, making visibility almost nil. I had backed off a deep drift, as the nose of the weasel was assuming an alarming angle, and then quite gently, it rolled on its side, decanting all its passengers into the snow. There was nothing we could do to right it, so we settled down on the lee side, and had lunch. Every now and then a skier loomed out of the mist, skinning up to the hut and stopped to sympathise. One, however, didn't stop, and I heard him say to his companion, as he passed, 'I really think it is going a bit far turning the weasel on its side to get shelter for lunch.' "

With the new tow Club members thought that they now had effortless uplift in store for the future, but this was an illusion. The tow had first to be cranked, which meant that not only was the engine to be turned over but also a massive gear and two hundred yards of rope. When finally the machine burst into life, skiers all around stopped in their climb up the hill and headed for the noise. To use the tow they had to grab the rope with one hand and hold on tight in order to maintain a locked grip. At this point a jet of water shot up the sleeve and uphill motion was achieved. To reach the bottom of the new tow members could take a lift in the weasel, but not all were enthusiastic about the new forms of uplift now available. The following letter appeared in the press: "On my first and probably last voyage in this perilous contraption – the weasel – I seated myself initially in a position where I was rapidly gassed. Rising for air I was thrown onto a portion of the vehicle which proceeded to scorch the seat of my trousers. Moving then to perch on one of its sides, I endured a

Opposite. The Scottish Ski Club ropetow on Beinn Glas, 1953. (L.R.S. Mackenzie)

process of being corrugated where previously I had been singed, till, reaching the limit of my endurance, I collapsed heavily onto a cleat on the floor. Before I could release my hand from under a nailed ski boot in order to rise, a roof stanchion collapsed, depositing three passengers who had been holding on to it, into the pit of my stomach. Without wishing to decry the efforts of those striving to solve the difficult problems of mechanisation, I ventured to suggest that as far as the Scottish Ski Club is concerned, painless elevation has yet to be achieved."

The Scottish Ski Club procured a second weasel and were pleased to report in 1951 that during the season they had conveyed 123 fare passengers and that the only casualty had been the treasurer who fell into a dead faint when told of the financial deficit on the operation. As the vehicle used one gallon of petrol per mile this was not surprising.

At Easter of that year one weasel was taken to Dalwhinnie for the club meet and used with great success at Drumochter. Deep consolidated snow made it possible to mount the steep shoulder of the Brackenalp of MacMurren Derby fame, above the Lodge. The weasel covered the distance from the road to the top in ten minutes and gave the skiers a run of 1,500 feet vertical descent. One enthusiast made three trips, thus establishing a record for downhill skiing in Scotland, in one day, 4,500 feet. The weasel was used again on Easter Sunday for the organisation of the Scottish Kandahar. The entry list of 69 included two Dominion and five foreign competitors. The club however only owned 45 racing bibs, so the weasel was delegated to ferry numbers for the late starters back to the top of the hill. In the event, just as it was needed most, it developed clutch trouble. Nevertheless as the press reported the following day: "the weasel added an air of importance to the race. Cameras, telephoto lenses and racing glasses as well as mechanical horsepower made the affair look very different from slap-happy Scottish Ski Race meetings of other years."

Lord Malcolm Douglas Hamilton had been invited to start the race but he refused to travel on the weasel. This caused a delay and racers had to start off at fifteen second intervals rather than thirty. As a result there was pandemonium at the last gate, which had been placed on the brink of a short, sharp, blind hollow. Racer after racer plunged down and fell over previous skiers who could not clear themselves out of the way. The Scottish Ski Club Journal reported that: "The crisis was reached as the 38th runner, N.D. Clark, of the home club, arrived in fine style, at high speed over the brink, to find fore-runners who had fallen in the preceding six seconds occupying all the available space, in, around, behind and before the finishing flag, inextricably knotted, immovable and indissoluble, one having a ski through another's number, and none

83

Bill Blackwood, inventor of several prototype ski tows.
(MacKenzie Album)

The Weasel in action.
(MacKenzie Album)

knowing which leg to saw off, but perchance it be his own. In a bold effort to clear the lot, Nobby was clocked in as the back of his neck came foremost through the flags, head down, feet up. As a reward, he achieved fourth place..." It had only been possible to use the weasel at this meeting because of the close proximity of the main road. Usually the Scottish Ski Club meet was held at Aviemore, and the Kandahar run in Coire Cas which was out of reach of a vehicle so extravagant on petrol.

One member of the Scottish Ski Club who was not satisfied with the weasel or the tow, decided to design his own uplift. William Blackwood produced many prototypes, the plans drawn in chalk on the back of his Edinburgh garage door. Donnaie MacKenzie remembers that when the machine eventually appeared, two years later: "It had a massive engine and looked like a raft with two lorry wheels and long shafts to guide it. There was no clutch and a pole forced the engine towards the drive shaft. At that point, the monster got under way and out of control. It was all right in Blackwood's garden, but on its first trial on the hill, this Frankenstein got its own back on its creator. It took off with three of us hanging to the shafts, and Willie trying to get level with the engine to switch off. Bodies flew in all directions as "Mark one" roared down the hill on its own and disappeared into a peat bog. All except Willie were for burying it where it lay."

Blackwood's "Mark two" was smaller, and this he erected on the Fiacaill òf Cairngorm. This proved to be another fiasco. Various tows followed, using broken down tractors, and tested in the field at Robert Allison's farm, at Turnhouse, just outside Edinburgh. Eventually Blackwood managed to procure an ex-army tracked vehicle. He had bought it at an auction sale in the north of England and drove it home complete with both twenty gallon petrol tanks full. Donnaie MacKenzie remembers that as far as he was concerned the petrol was the only merit pertaining to this vehicle which occupied all of his skiing time with struggles to maintain it moving in the right direction. Blackwood did not give up, and by the following year had procured a Studebaker staff car. Some members of the Scottish Ski Club particularly Philip Rankin and the Watson family of Helensburgh suggested to him that a real challenge would be to erect a tow on Meall a' Bhuiridh in Glencoe, rather than persevere in the Cairngorms. Donnaie MacKenzie was there when this idea was put into effect: "Blackwood always seemed to gather a happy and insanely dedicated band of helpers, and they were on full parade for the operation to get the Studebaker to a position of Meall a' Bhuiridh, about a thousand yards below the summit. At the wheel of the car was a part-time racing driver and pulling was one tracked vehicle with another on the downhill side hopefully to prevent the convoy from

Members of the Scottish Ski Club
struggle with the engine for a Bill
Blackwood tow.
(MacKenzie Album)

rolling down the hill. The wheels of the Studebaker frequently disappeared out of sight and had to be levered up with very inadequate bits of wood. Eventually, it shot out of the bog with wheels spinning and the leverers diving for cover. Ross McLean stayed too long at his post on one occasion and received a large piece of Meall a' Bhuiridh on the kisser.

The operation took two days and the final traverse entailed building a hundred yards of track across a steep slope. It was only Blackwood who knew how 'Mark three' was going to work on site. We eventually discovered it was to drive a wire rope on a drum fixed in place of a rear wheel with an opposing lay wheel as a tensioning device. The rope actually went to the top of the mountain being supported by three legged pylons which sat on top of the snow. The skier attached himself to the rope with a pole with a hook on the end, rather like the tool for lopping high branches off trees. It was a great day when the rope actually started to move uphill and disappeared out of sight over the crest. The first of the happy band attached themselves to the rope with the long poles and moved up. Had gravity finally been conquered? It had for one or two, until disaster struck. Somehow, the return rope had got fankled in a pulley at the top, unknown to the engine operator. The top pylon proceeded downhill, collecting its brothers en route and the operator only knew all was not well when a load of pylons came charging over the crest and downhill at him. It was a sad moment for Blackwood because he knew he had to go back to the drawing board – or in his case, the back of his garage door. Meanwhile, professionals were moving in and 'Mark three, Blackwood' suffered the final indignity of being dynamited to make roon for the 'real' thing.''

It is interesting to reflect that the "real thing" was the prototype Pomagalsi lift designed by the managing director of British Ropeway Engineering Company at the cost of £2,500 plus many hundreds of hours labour by ski club members. At the start of 1950, skiers in Scotland could travel on a tracked weasel from the valley to the snow and could buy a season ticket on a rope tow. They could also now buy petrol, and it was the return of this commodity that opened up a variety of new fields to the Scottish weekend skiers. Previously distance had limited them to the Killin area or Glenshee, but now they could travel as far as the Cairngorms or Glencoe for the weekend.

The army had discovered the potential of Scottish skiing during the war. But it was Montgomery who saw that there was also a place for it as peace-time sport. He felt that with National Service continuing, the army had a chance of introducing skiing to a large part of the youth of the country. Colonel Grant of Rothiemurchus offered the army a site near the Lairig Ghru on which to build a hut, where he imagined there would be a relaxed atmosphere with no military discipline or rank. Monty jumped at this opportunity, but had reservations about abandoning rank. "However" he remarked to Colonel Grant, "One has to have rank, of course, in order to have something to abandon." He agreed with Colonel Grant that there was a tremendous future for winter sports in Scotland where he had skied on many occasions before the war with the Ski Club of Great Britain. The Nuffield Trust was approached to finance the building of a hut and it was agreed that it would be done on "Toc H" lines. With Monty moving the wires in the War Office, it was quickly erected. The army immediately formed a Ski Association, membership being 3/6d per year.

When the weekend civilian skiers heard of this, there was consternation. Nearly all their equipment had been bought in ex-army shops at rock bottom prices. "Heavens" one secretary is reported to have said "Many members of my club will find their haversacks, webb equipment; anti-gas jackets; B.D. jerkins, leather; and even their very trousers claimed by their rightful owners."

The official opening of the army hut is remembered by William McLaren of the Dundee Ski Club. He had caught the train in Perth at 6 a.m. and as he alighted in Aviemore, he remembers that: "Awaiting us were jeeps galore, but the drivers had no sure idea of our destination – a log hut somewhere in the Lairig Ghru. I showed them the way. It was a familiar enough route to me, up the Morlich road, though snow-bound for a change, then we were ceremoniously directed off through the trees by an immaculate M.P. to follow a blazed trail, till another of his colleagues appeared like a genie from the snow and pine clad wilderness and made us dismount, and I reluctantly got out. Now came a long weary trudge up through the snow, in places, barely heather deep. Skis seem less disabling worn on foot than shoulder, but people now began to pass us. First a kilted officer with wellington boots then a pipe major carrying a suitcase. Finally, a couple of civilians with walking sticks who made the issue clear – the planks were shouldered again. At last, a wisp of smoke through the trees and our objective gradually became tangible against the side of Castle Hill. A fine sturdy structure too, was this Scottish Command Recreational Ski Headquarters in the Cairngorms but my thoughts were not now aesthetic, but of that painful, empty organ beneath my belt. With ne'er a word, I staggered up the steps and into the pleasant warmth. A couple of officers were seated at the table with the plans of the imminent operation before them. They looked up with glances signifying pained regret at my arrival, rather than congratulations on my achievement, "Not yet old boy, please. The place hasn't been officially opened. Why not try skiing? There's a patch of snow behind the hut." With my seven hour appetite, I turned numbly out into the snow. It was coming down as well. I found an assortment of skiers disporting on a small drift and, after what seemed an interminable wait, more senior officers came marching briskly over the brow of the ridge and with them the gracious lady who was to honour the hut with her opening touch. We gathered quickly in the forecourt and watched with polite silence as the door through which I had made my brief sortie so long before, adamantly refused to open. However, the clerk of works, a powerful man, soon dealt with the problem and the platform party was followed in by those from the winter auditorium.

A generous plying with sherry and my "vittles" were soon playing a merry overture. A fine meal of roast venison followed. I never imagined that I would attend a four course meal served by white jacketed waiters in the midst of a snow storm in the Lairig Ghru.

Soon the port was circulating and then the conversation, and the music of the pipes. The lady of honour, duly presented with a gift of a cigarette box, whimsically remarked on the happy concurrence of the original and postponed dates of the event, due to continual snow storms. This had permitted the inscription to be altered from 5th to 15th December, with but a stroke of the needle!

It was late in the afternoon when we reluctantly departed from the warm and friendly sanctuary. Again, an attempt was made to ski, but efforts this time were foiled, as much by lack of the finer sense of equilibrium, as of snow. Soon my kindly companion on the path was insisting on carrying my ski; he being the laird of this land and an ex-Commando Colonel, I didn't put up too much resistance. Soon we were back on the trail and jeeping into the valley and an end of a memorable day with the officers."

The army now had somewhere to stay; but so too, did civilians. Glenmore Lodge had been bought by the Central Council for Physical Recreation. It was opened on September the 6th 1947, by the Secretary of State for Scotland who declared, "The aim of the centre is to make available for all sections of the community, the joys of the open air, using the mountains, the glens and the loch." It was hoped that courses covering a wide variety of subjects would be conducted with particular emphasis on training scout, guide and student leaders so that they could return to their groups and pass on their new found information on botany, hill walking, snow craft, climbing and, of course, skiing. As was said at the time, "There are so many from our great cities and towns who would like to get the thrill of the high places, but who need guidance. It is hoped there will be an ever widening circle of keen club men and women who will come forward to help with this task. It may be that, as a result of the co-operation of all centred here at the Lodge, a future generation in our land will look to the high places and the open air for their recreation."

The courses to be held at the Lodge by the "Physical Wrecks" as the C.C.P.R. were termed irreverently, were for a week, and cost £5. By an arrangement with the Dundee Ski Club anyone applying through their secretary could receive a week's course in skiing only, but had to fall in with other activities in the event of there being no snow.

Life at the Lodge started at 8 a.m. with breakfast, then every one set off for the snow. At times skiing could be enjoyed at the Lodge itself but usually the venue was Coire Cas. After a one and a half hour's walk, the party would reach Jean's hut, where they ate a second breakfast. This small shelter had been erected in 1952 by the father of Jean Smith who was killed while skiing in Coire Cas in 1948. It was intended as a temporary refuge that was open to all. A brew of cocoa was handed out here and then classes were marshalled and instruction commenced. The morning was given over to lessons and then after lunch the pupils were encouraged to ski on their own. The day's exercise over, the objective was now to reach the Lodge before the tea-trolley was removed from the lounge. After the evening meal the exhausted skiers joined together for a ceilidh. As one pupil remembers: "A week's course soon passed and on Aviemore station many farewells were taken among people who had come together, worked hard and learnt a new sport in the surroundings of the Cairngorms."

One of the instructors was Dickie Gower, a veteran climber and skier, and a committee member of the Maryhill Youth Club. He and his fellow Creag Dhu Club member, Jack Thomson, arrived at the Lodge soon after its opening and were invited to become instructors. Jack had fought in Yugoslavia and Greece, and after this had found his trade as shoemaker in Glasgow somewhat boring. Instead he had worked as a handyman at Ardvorlich Camp on Loch Sloy, where he had ample opportunity to climb and ski. With Jean, his new bride, he moved into the disused game larder at the Lodge and devoted his time to improving the standard of "Glenmorons" as pupils at the Lodge were affectionately called. With Glenmore Lodge and the opening of the army hut, the fulcrum of Scottish skiing was now firmly established in Spey Valley. Not around Newtonmore and Drumochter as before the war but in the northern corries of the Cairngorms.

6. "THIS IS THE JINKY'S"

Opposite. The Lomonds and Creagdhu Mountaineering Clubs were at the heart of skiing in Glencoe. Front row from left, Jeannie and Frith Finlayson and Helen Carmichael. (Finlayson Album)

"Scottish skiing is in that awkward stage between pigtails and perms, when lemonade is no longer good enough and our legs cannot stand cocktails" wrote Philip Rankin, editor of the Scottish Ski Club Journal in 1952. He realised that for the sport to develop, better uplift facilities were essential, but at present these were beyond the resources of a small club. In an effort to increase membership and possibly generate the capital required, the club published a booklet titled, "Skiing in Scotland". It assessed Scottish snow, weather and facilities and included a list of available huts. The editor stated: "The Cairngorms above all need extensive development of hut accommodation, alas none yet exists, nor does it seem likely that there will until the general popularity of the sport brings larger numbers of people to Scotland. The extensive erection and maintenance is at present beyond the combined resources of the ski clubs and there is no other organisation likely to interest itself in the foreseeable future."

The booklet drew attention to the fact that accidents in Scotland were extremely rare, due to the degree of fitness induced by the effort of climbing. It was suggested that while only a small first aid kit need be carried, a screwdriver, strong string and sticky tape were useful for constructing a stretcher from ski sticks and skins. Skiers had to be able to look after themselves. Readers were encouraged to walk to the summit of Cairngorm, from where they could descend on two runs both over 2 miles in length. Braeriach was also recommended with four excellent routes back down to the valley. The highest rating was reserved for Meall a' Bhuiridh. "The main run is perhaps the finest individual one in the country and it is well worth climbing to the summit for the superb view alone." The booklet was so successful that several editions were published over subsequent years.

The majority of the Scottish Ski Club had meanwhile abandoned Ben Lawers and the Killin area in favour of Meall a' Bhuiridh in Glencoe. They were not the first however, the Creag Dhu Mountaineering Club had been skiing there since 1938. An association of hard rock and ice climbers from Clydeside, the club was formed in the Depression of the 1920s when the jobless artisans and heavy manual workers from the shipyards and engineering factories had gathered at Craigallian, a remote spot midway between the Kilpatrick and Campsie Hills. There they sat around a fire and talked, but were soon looking for action, which they found in the hills. Having no maps or guide books and little money, they had to teach themselves to "live off the land". They climbed on the Whangie and Cobbler, then moved north to Glencoe where they put up a series of climbs far in advance of anything that had been done before. When the faces were unclimbable, owing to bad weather, they utilised the time by walking further into the hills and on these journeys gained a wide knowledge of bothies and "dosses".

Ba Cottage was such a doss. When the new road through Glencoe was opened in 1932, Ba was left on an isolated loop and this became their headquarters. Chris Lyon first stayed there in 1935 and he remembers that there were two books handed round to everyone to read who stayed there overnight, written by the Marchioness of Breadalbane, about stalking and grouse shooting on the Black Mount. Chris recollects that the first person to actually mention skis in the doss was Alexander Muir. He had been called up in 1938 to serve in the militia, but in order to avoid drill had volunteered for special training to fight in Finland during the Finnish-Russian war. His unit was posted to the French Alps for winter training and being known as a top mountaineer, labelled by the Creag Dhu as "the Iron Man", he soon became friendly with a French mountain instructor who taught him how to ski. The officer in charge of the unit though, objected to this relationship. Alex "banjoed" him, which resulted in jail and a court martial. He had however learned to ski and when he eventually arrived home he gathered up a small group of friends and headed for the west, intending to teach them his new craft.

Most outdoor clubs had folded for the duration of the war, but the Creag Dhu managed to carry on with a small band of teenage apprentice engineers and older men working in the shipyards and factories. They procured guns which helped them to live off the land and they used their engineering skills to make climbing and ski equipment. During the exceptionally severe winters of the forties they had skied on the Kilpatrick Hills and Campsies with a few holidays spent in the Cairngorms. Chris Lyon remembers that: "A typical long day's skiing for us in the 'Gorms in 1942 would be to backpack a week's food to Ryvoan then up at 7 a.m. and skim over Mam Suim to Cairngorm, then up to MacDhui and return via Carn Lochan and the Lurcher's Gully. We would have a big fire and drum up at Clach Bharig and then ski back to Ryvoan for supper. From the German prisoner of war camp near

Loch Morlich we would get fresh bread. Ski instruction could easily be obtained for a few cigarettes.

Once I was accosted by a sergeant who came up to me and my friend Bob Clyde and asked us if we would instruct some of the troops. Bob and I laughed like drains. We could not take seriously the idea of troops skiing for anything but sport."

The Creag Dhu would have preferred to ski in Glencoe, but the only means of transport, MacBrayne's bus – demanded priority war-work passes and would not permit skis aboard. By 1944 however, the Government had eased restrictions to allow occasional charter buses to be run for "cultural outdoor activities", by approved groups. The Creag Dhu immediately began to run a regular club bus. Chris Lyon recollects: "The young Creag Dhu zealots considered playing around on skis was fine when the snow lay thick in the woods, moors and glens, but it was a waste of time when the snows consolidated firm enough to climb. Skiing also had a 'posh' image, therefore it was thought to be a wee bit Jessie, to the hard cases on the bus.

Bob Clyde was the first man to brass neck carting a pair of children's skis onto the bus. He climbed to the top of Ben Lui, convinced in the theory that 'if it can be glissaded, then it can be skied'. He hurtled down in a series of spectacular cartwheels, spat out the snow at the foot of the corrie and screamed 'This is the Jinky's!' Within a few weekends, slings and karabiners were being transformed into a hanging rack for a dozen pairs of skis on the bus; their owners being changed from ice-tigers to downhill shussboomers. Ba Cottage, the doss – East Ridge and Ba Corrie, Meall a' Bhuiridh the slopes – word of this howff and the new breakneck sport quickly spread, and some of the young Lomond hard tickets joined in. We were also joined by Peter McGeoch, who had worked in the forestry in the Glencoe area, in the early years of the war, before working abroad with the Crown Agents."

Parallel to the Creag Dhu were the Lomonds, established in 1930. The members of this association were mostly teachers and technicians. By 1938 they had become a well organised mountaineering club with rooms of their own in Glasgow. They were the first club to charter a regular bus for weekend excursions and although there was always a strong rivalry between the Lomonds and Creag Dhu, a few seats were always reserved for the Creag Dhu on their bus. Some of the Lomonds ventured into ski mountaineering and as the equipment was expensive they began manufacturing skis and bindings in their club rooms. Chris Lyon remembers that he was of importance in this undertaking as his job of apprentice engineer enabled him to procure the necessary pieces of pigskin used to make the ski bindings. By the 1950s both clubs had buses running to Glencoe.

Late on a Saturday night they would drop off their skiing passengers at Loch Ba. If the Lomond and Creag Dhu arrived at the same time a frantic cross country race with skis and full weekend rucksacks would commence across the two miles of peat hags, the winner claiming the best places in the doss. Then, having dumped their heavy gear the men would set out for the Ba woods and return with armfulls of fuel for a large fire. Because of the age old rivalry between the clubs, these races were becoming more vicious until a truce was called and a room allocated to each group, with stragglers allowed the space between. Instead of a mad rush across the moor, the two clubs could now be seen forming a long crocodile as they wended their way towards the bothy singing, although sometimes, if the buses had stayed too long at the Tyndrum Bar, this orderly procession could resemble Napoleon's retreat from Moscow.

Happy days at Ba cottage came to an end with its destruction by fire. Seeking new shelter the skiers moved round to the base of the hill and found their way into Blackrock Cottage, Some of the Lomond roofed over an old sheep fank as an alternative while other members of the Creag Dhu tended to go further and erected a canvas doss after the style of a tinker's humpy. Tents and other shanties sprang up in the back meadow of the cottage itself. Chris Lyon remembers that: "A normal day's skiing would be to cart skis, rucksacks, primus stove and 'drum up' gear to Island Rock at the foot of the main basin, on Meall a' Bhuiridh, and from there the skis would be carried to the summit. Ten times for ten downhill runs. Then a last hike to the summit and ski to the road, via three routes, which we called the Main Basin, Spring Run or Etive Glades. There was always the occasional epic. On one glorious spring evening, a bunch of stalwarts were resting at the tents at Black Rock meadow, having that day climbed from there to the summit and skied down four times. Some wag suggested a race – entry fee, one cigarette – prize winner take all; rules being that the twenty or so contestants would climb back to the summit for the fifth time that day. One, two, three, GO! First to touch the shed door at Black Rock, the winner. Each of the contestants had worked out the best route down on the long slog up, but were horrified when they saw one of their number, small Harry McKay, take off in the Main Basin in a straight shuss, roaring into the gully, and rocketing out thirty feet above the snow in a straight line. On the long slide across the plateau, the heavier, stronger racers, overtook Harry and picked their own line downhill, then gasped in amazement when they observed him hurtling down, straight as an

The Doss built at the foot of Meall a'
Bhuiridh.
(Finlayson Album)

Inside the Doss, Frith Finlayson and Bill
Smith.
(Finlayson Album)

arrow, to romp across the tent filled meadow as easy winner. Well-wishers congratulated wee Harry for his dare-devil descent. 'Were you not frightened?' queried a young lady. He replied that 'Because I was the youngest and smallest, therefore the most trustworthy among that bunch of hard cases, I got to hold the 22 cigarette prize. I was so terrified at the summit, I unconsciously lit a fag, then smoked two more on the plateau, and I had no cigarettes to make up for this deficit, so if someone else had won the race, that bunch of animals would have nailed me to the stable door like an old hooded craw on a gamekeeper's vermin fence. I had to win!'

About this period of time, the Ladies Mountaineering Club obtained a long term lease of Blackrock Cottage. On the first good ski day, they were aghast to find their quiet mountain retreat surrounded by tents and shanties. With the feminine gusto that they applied to everything they tackled, the ladies bought a new broom and proceeded to clear the trash. The first two attempts were complete failures. Personal contact with the roughnecks only brought rebuff. Time and money were spent in constructing a stout steel padlocked gate at the main road. These were repeatedly dismantled and carried further and further into the moor. The ladies then decided on chemical warfare. They brought in the sanitary inspector, and, backed by the full arm of the law, the campers and dossers were at last cleared, and Granny's Heilan' Hame was saved.

However, some of the Lomonds visited Black Mount and found the landlord, Major Fleming very displeased that the ladies' high-handed action should bring a government snooper sniffing around his private kingdom. He gave the Lomond team permission to utilise the old sheep fank as a temporary shelter, and intimated that he would like to meet the Creag Dhu to give them a similar offer. They, as a club had no wish to acquire property, nor worldly goods, and so ignored this gesture, but some time later, over a dram with the gamekeeper, without anything being said officially, they agreed to accept a site for a shack, the terms being that the roof must come off from May until December. The Creag Dhu decided as a club that the doss they already had at the foot of the Buchaille, called Jacksonville, was sufficient to their needs, so a small number only of the Creag Dhu took up the keeper's offer. As they dug out the foundations, Frith Finlayson approached the small team and suggested that as he and others were now roofless, why did we not pool our skill and materials and build one good shanty? That night in the King's House bar, it was stated that as there were only two dosses left, and that each of these were officially disowned by their parent clubs, we the skiers should form a new club, but even among this very small group, agreement could not be reached. Someone suggested that as the

Frith Finlayson, he set up his own ski school in Glencoe.
(Finlayson Album)

Setting off from the Doss from left, Bill Smith, Harry McKay, Frith Finlayson and his son Ian.
(Finlayson Album)

Creag Dhu owned the biggest doss, we should be called the 'Big Crowd'. The Lomonds retorted thrawnily 'Then we are the Wee Crowd'. From the Big Crowd sprang the Glencoe Ski Club, and from the Wee Crowd the White Corries Rescue Patrol. By the mid fifties, mingled with the raucous, ribald voices of the Clydeside pioneers, could be heard the genteel accents of Kelvinside and Milngavie. The Scottish Ski Club had arrived in force". Friendships, though, were soon formed among both groups. The exuberance of the survivors of the Glasgow Industrial Revolution was immediately apparent to the newcomers.

The "Big Crowd's" doss was upgraded through the years and became known as the Palace and was the centre of social life for all the various camps, tents and caravans, that fore-gathered in the area over the weekends. Frith Finlayson soon became the fastest speaker and leading enthusiast. He had stood on skis for the first time dressed in his winter climbing clothes — boots and all — between two good friends, who were to be his prospective instructors. He remembers that: "Being one of a group of young who at that time did everything the hard way, I naturally was to be taught the parallel Christie. My first instructions were as follows: 'Point your ski straight down the hill, holding yourself back with the points of your sticks dug into the snow in front of you. To Christie to the right, you move off, gain speed and bend down over the left ski, straighten up quickly then down over your right ski, and that's all there is to it.'"

Frith felt that there must be a better way to learn. He was determined to master the sport. He appreciated that the length of skis should suit the user's height, and that ski sticks should be chest high with the basket resting on the snow. Detail was all important to Frith and soon his friends began to realise that his advice was worth listening to. Except for those in the army, Scottish skiers had usually gone abroad for their instruction, but Frith, with his Glasgow confidence, now set up his own school in Glencoe. With his engineering background, precision was all important, so his clients were expected to look smart as well as carrying out his instructions implicitly. This was a new idea to the khaki clad crash-and-bash brigade of skiers to be found on the Scottish hills.

While Glasgow skiers tended to congregate at Glencoe, the Edinburgh section of the Scottish Ski Club favoured the Cairngorms. Both groups felt that in order to get the best from their skiing, there must be development, with civilised access, lifts, accommodation and shelter. They knew that Scotland was trailing far behind, having neither the commercial type of continental resort, nor the private type of development, that by this time was booming in North America, Australia, New Zealand and Canada.

Creagdhu hard rock climbers: From left, Frith Finlayson, Bill Smith, Johnnie Cunningham and Harry McKay.
(Finlayson Album)

7. BRAIDS TO BRECO

More and more skiers were attracted to the Alps each year to the detriment of trade in Norway. In an attempt to reverse this trend the Norwegian government sponsored an exhibition of ski jumping on the Braid Hills near Edinburgh. An artificial jump was constructed from tubular scaffolding and snow was specially imported by sea from Norway. As lorries laden with melting snow passed through the city on their way from Leith Docks, interest in the event quickened. Tickets for the stand that had been erected on the 7th tee of the golf course, were quickly sold out. The event was to start on a Friday evening. The weather was fair and an enormous crowd made their way to the Braid Hills to watch. Army searchlights illuminated the jump. The run-out started on snow but the competitors had to finish on straw. After a few jumps one bystander was heard to remark that he had seen "at least one Norwegian whose finish resembled a combine-harvester at work, emerging from the straw in a series of hay fever explosions". The competition continued on the Saturday by which time the scaffolding was obscured by sleet, driven before a strong wind, which lent an air of authenticity to the scene. The wind blew in violent gusts across the jump. It was biting cold and the sleet turned to ice as it hit the metal scaffolding. The winner of the event was Arne Hoel, with a jump of 36 metres. He received the Caledonian Cup, a trophy presented by the Scottish Norwegian Society, to be competed for annually in Scotland. The Scottish Ski Club held a party in the evening for the visiting Norwegians. A bottle of whisky per head was consumed and the event considered a success. Out of this contact came an annual return visit by members of the Ski Club which continued for fifteen years.

Glenshee was growing in popularity as a place to ski. Rivalry had sprung up between the Dundee Ski Club and the Perth section of the Scottish Ski Club, who both gathered in the same area. In January of 1949, they decided to hold a competition. It was to be a casual event without most of the things usually considered necessary for ski racing, such as, "snow, flags, stop-watches, officials and other causes of delay".

This was such a success that all sections of the two clubs decided to come together to compete in a relay race, each running simultaneously with a geschmozzle start.

This idea was later modified to a knock-out event run in heats. Mr. C.D.G. Tennant, the Perth convener, offered to organise a tournament and generously agreed to present a challenge trophy which he delivered in a brown paper parcel to the race committee of the Scottish Ski Club, along with a letter which read: "I am a bit self-conscious about the piece of plate because my wife has already tried to get rid of it at various jumble sales, and white elephant stalls and it has always been returned with thanks. I can only think that it has been preserved by some divine providence for this great event." When the parcel was unwrapped it was seen to contain a very odd silver ornament, which was later identified as an epergne, a Victorian centre piece. To compete for the trophy each team was to be made up of eight runners of whom at least two must be ladies, and one a veteran. The contest was to be run on knock-out lines, the two teams running simultaneously, the only control being the finish judges flag, which would be the signal to send off the next runner of a team. Competitors had to finish with at least one ski attached to the foot and an additional rule stated that "false starts, throwing ski and biting, gouging and scratching in clinches at gates, shall be considered fouls".

The Tennant trophy soon became the most discussed and anticipated event in the racing calendar. The first course consisted of four open gates, followed by a sharp shuss, running out in the last thirty yards to an uphill icy rise on top of which was the finishing post with a large banner proclaiming "ZIEL", the equivalent Gaelic word not being known. In the ensuing battle this area was the scene of many spectacular falls, as the slight upturn was not noticeable in the flat grey light and unsteady racers were immediately tipped over backwards, one remarked that "without forward velocity it was virtually impossible to make any further progress up the sheet of polished ice to the finishing flag without crampons or an ice axe". Excitement grew to fever pitch in the duel between women competitors from Perth and Glasgow: "One lady stuck grimly to her skis through a series of magnificent schuss-bums, passing her opponent on the schusses and being passed in the other attitude, while her opponent gradually shed her equipment piecemeal around the countryside. Both her skis had arrived at the finish by the time she herself had reached the final schuss, and exhorted by bellows of 'Run' she commenced a series of what may best be described as rotating glissades, in pursuit of the enemy who was by this time yawing furiously down the schuss like a runaway windmill. Hope of her survival was small and only just fulfilled and she had barely a yard or two of lead left as she emerged from her grave of icebergs. Had the lady on foot been in better training, undoubtedly, she would have won by her eyelashes against the skier, who slid back one pace for every two forward to the finish. As it was, it was a dead heat, and the next runners even."

While the majority of Scottish skiers congregated together there were still some who preferred to tour and to set off in small groups into the hinterland. At the New Year of 1953 the violent weather, with driving snow, kept most skiers close to the road. A group of the Lomond club, however, set off for Corrour bothy. From there they intended to climb Ben Alder but were overcome by a blizzard of such intensity, that three of them died from exposure and exhaustion, a grim reminder of the severity of the Scottish winter.

There was little alternative to Scotland though, for any Scots who wanted to ski. The foreign currency allowance had fallen again and was now down to £25. Pressure from ski club members for better uplift facilities increased. Philip Rankin put forward a proposal to the Scottish Ski Club that they should put up £2,000 and allow him a free hand to go ahead with his plans for the erection of a proper tow on Meall a' Bhuiridh. He persuaded the club to abandon the home-made tow which Bill Blackwood was still pursuing and adopt his much more ambitious and expensive proposal.

Members of the club were asked for donations and the first to contribute was founder member George Donald who remarked that, at 84, he was doubtful if he could ever get the full value out of a season ticket on the tow, but hoped that his money might speed the process up for his sake. The landowner, Major Fleming raised no objections to a tow provided it was not of permanent construction and that the working party who were to erect it were off the hill by the end of July, in order to give the grouse a time of peace and quiet before the shooting season.

The prime movers in this undertaking were Philip Rankin, Lewis Drysdale and Robert Finlay, although the ultimate responsibility for accepting the challenge, and calling on Scottish Ski Club members to entrust them with a substantial sum of money, lay with the President, Colonel H.J. Butchart. The schedule was very tight. Breco, the firm who were to make the tow, required the order to be placed by May 1st 1955 if they were to deliver by the end of June. Before that, they required a full survey of the slope, and the completion of both the preparatory work on access and the aerial ropeway for the final construction. All the materials for foundation work, had also to be on the site before the tow arrived. Concrete foundations were to be laid on the basis of a drawing that was yet to be received. Philip Rankin remembers that: "By the last weekend in April, by fair means and foul, we seemed to have tapped ready cash to a standstill once again, still £1,200 short of the target of £5,000, without which we felt it was not safe to proceed.

The situation was saved when two members undertook to provide half in cash as a prior loan, providing the club would guarantee the other half out of its reserves in order to cover the estimated costs without further delay. This suggestion was approved by the committee, and after a few signings and speeches, the assembly retired to celebrate the occasion suitably, dropping the order for the tow into the letter box outside the secretary's office as they went. The date was April 29th, almost exactly the fourth birthday of the great idea conjured out of a blue sky shining on the Island Rock. The peace of the neighbourhood was shattered the next week by the first stick of 'geely' going off on the access track to shift an awkward rock."

Luckily for the club, the summer of 1955 was extremely dry. So little rain had fallen in fact, that, at the Glasgow Fair, there was not enough water ready to hand for mixing concrete. However, with club members doing the ground work the track was improved to allow a six-wheeled lorry to make the journey to the commencement of an aerial ropeway. The materials were then shuttled across the plateau by "weasels", at which point another ropeway of 150 yards long was strung across the final escarpment, and bags of sand, gravel and cement were soon sailing through the air. An enormous amount of equipment had to be hauled up this "Blondin", as the work party called it, after the French tightrope walker who crossed the Niagara Falls, before the real work of laying the foundations could even begin. Unexpected difficulties had to be solved, and more manpower brought in, but the ground preparations were completed by the end of June by which time parts of the tow began to arrive. Philip Rankin recollects "The first bits were the poles for the tripods, each one was a stout lift on level ground for four men, and there were forty five of them, plus to each tripod a hundred and more bits of assorted odds and ends. One of the near disasters occurred with four of these poles on their way up the ropeway. Just as the load was nearing the top, the order was given to 'heave' and we did so with such good effect that with a loud 'twank' the rope parted. Four eighteen foot organ pipes went shooting back whence they came, giving clear and audible warning of their progress. It is claimed that no stag ever covered the ground on Meall a' Bhuiridh as fast as the foreman down below as he saw his consignment returning 'expresso'. The rope had fallen victim to the system of returning the running carriage from the top. With two hundred and fifty yards of rope to haul down behind it, the empty carriage had to be loaded with a large knob of Argyll, whereupon it went fizzing back to base, with rope whipping around like a demented serpent

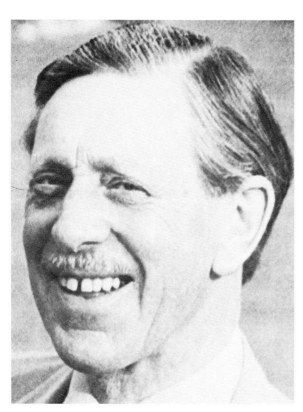

Philip Rankin, the driving force behind
the development of skiing in Glencoe.
(M.R. Kenneth)

Bill Smith, a member of the working
party, in 1957 at Glencoe he skied
34,000 feet downhill in one day, the first
"Everest" on a Scottish hill.
(M.R. Kenneth)

along the tow path. The consequence was quite a fair sized cairn at the foot of the ropeway and had the task gone on long enough, one can only conclude the contour of the mountain would have been reversed, the ski tow ultimately going downhill. The only damage done was to one pole which was riveted up in the shape of a snake charmer's tooter."

The site manager for Breco, Mr. Taylor, arrived on the first weekend in July. Bad weather set in and his enthusiasm for Scotland fell significantly. His last ski tow project had been in Colorado, at Jasper Park, where he had Red Indians to work as navvies. Here he had to make do with the Creag Dhu and the Lomond work party and Paddy Heron's men from Fort William. Mr. Heron had told the Scottish Ski Club that an erector and four men could do the job in three or four weeks, but Philip Rankin was sceptical, and was not surprised when it became obvious that they were falling behind schedule.

British Ropes gave the rope for the tow free as it was regarded an experiment and they sent up two of their men to do the splice; this job involved joining two lengths of forty feet rope in such a way that it would be invisible and not alter the gauge of the remaining cable. Time was running out fast. By July 20th, Major Fleming's deadline for the work party to be off the hill, it seemed as if just one more week might allow the job to be accomplished. This was allowed, but advantage could not be taken of the extra time, as at that very moment the contractor's men went down with a bad attack of food poisoning.

The Scottish Ski Club had been amazingly lucky in the generosity of the landlord, who had permitted the club to do almost anything that they wanted on his land. Free tenure had been granted for a minimum period of ten years and conditions were few. The club was also fortunate that Breco looked upon the tow as of special significance to illustrate their product in Scotland and did not treat it as a normal commercial proposition. The makers of the diesel engine, Lister, considered it an experimental project, as the site was higher than any they had used before. That they were prepared to test their equipment in a place with the worst weather conditions in Britain and to leave it under the care of amateurs rather than qualified engineers, was perhaps surprising. The greatest piece of luck though, was the fact that Mr. Heron of Fort William was a member of the Ski Club and was determined to carry out the project within the limited time. Philip Rankin remarked that: "On his own head, he took the hazards of Glencoe, the Scottish climate, and the clottish committee in trying to do what was nearly a public works contract on a private club budget. It is probable that on a commercial basis, the contracting cost alone would have far exceeded the total cost of the whole project — a fact of which Mr. Heron was no doubt very well aware before he started. For the moment, the Scottish Ski Club lion may continue to wag his tail in the air. Scottish skiing is on the march, even if we hope that means exactly the opposite of what it says."

It was the drive and money of a small core of members of the Scottish Ski Club that built the tow. Chris Lyon remembered that when many of the pioneers in his group first saw this new monstrosity desecrating their hill, their immediate decision was to get rid of the eyesore. One free run however and the next thought was "how can we get in on the act?"

It was announced in the Journal of the Scottish Ski Club for 1956 that the new tow was in operation. It had a capacity of 250 skiers per hour giving a lift of 900 feet. Members were reminded that power was supplied by diesel engine and the tow operated at speeds of about six miles per hour. "Here is, at last, the means whereby serious continuous practice in ski running and ski teaching may be undertaken without the excessive fatigue involved in climbing. The ultimate result on the general standard of skiing in Scotland can hardly be held in doubt. Details of the organisation must still be regarded as provisional, but the following points should be noted by all skiers wishing to enjoy the use of Glencoe ski tow.

1. The tow is owned and operated by the Scottish Ski Club, solely for members.

2. Tickets for the use of the tow can only be obtained from the Control Committee by post.

3. Persons not normally resident in Scotland, may become temporary members at slightly reduced rates annually. Such members are entitled to enjoy the normal facilities offered by the club.

4. An additional facility which will be offered to members on the mountain will be the storage of ski in the club hut erected beside the tow. A small charge will be made."

A proof of the usefulness of the tow was that in 1957, one member of the tow party, Bill Smith, skied 34,000 feet in one day − 17 miles of "downhill only" − the first Everest on a Scottish hill.

8. CAIRNGORMS

The Glencoe and Glenshee ski tows were built by skiers for skiers. In the Cairngorms the need for uplift was solved in a different manner. There had been considerable changes there since 1896 when the Cairngorm Club warned its members: "Although Aviemore is a favourite starting point for the Cairngorms, unfortunately it has, at present, no hotel and there is no accommodation of any kind for passing tourists. When the direct route to the Highland railway from Aviemore to Inverness is opened, a hotel may possibly be built to meet the increased requirements of so important a junction."

By the 1950s several hotels stayed open to cater for skiers. At the Nethybridge Hotel, Jock Kerr Hunter ran ski classes throughout the winter. He felt strongly that his instruction would be far more effective if his pupils did not have to expend so much energy in walking uphill. Realising that he could not build ski tows himself, he approached the Central Council for Physical Recreation and suggested that the council should gather together a group of people interested in developing some sort of uplift for the large number of skiers now gathering in Coire Cas.

As spokesman for this newly formed group, Kerr Hunter, stated in December 1954 that "we feel that winter sports has now grown big enough in the Cairngorms to warrant some sort of facility". To his surprise his statement was met by stiff opposition. Some hoteliers felt that it was a personal insult. They considered that the services they were producing were adequate and were quite unwilling to exert effort or spend any money in improving them. Scottish skiers however, felt otherwise. A letter to the press at the time pointed out that: "It will not come amiss to remind the hoteliers in the Cairngorm area that even the smallest and cheapest pensions in Switzerland regard hot water, clean boots, adequate packed lunches, table service and willingness to oblige, as normal. It is alas, not necessarily the cheapest of pensions around the Cairngorms with whom we make the comparison. Currently, Scottish skiers are engaged in doing something which will benefit hotels – maybe creating a trade at a time when now there is little, and often none. In the new edition of 'Skiing in Scotland', old routes into once popular parts of the Cairngorms are marked 'now impassable to vehicles'. King Canute could not keep the tide from rolling, but a lesson or two in the working of a Swiss resort might show the Cairngorm hoteliers how to stop the tide rolling out."

Jock Kerr Hunter stressed to the District Clerk in Kingussie, Roddie MacLean, that the skiers brought in to the Spey Valley at least £10,000 during the months of March and April, and that anything that could be done to keep them in the area would be well worthwhile. "I can assure you," he added, "that at the moment there is a definite feeling amongst skiers towards moving their headquarters to Glencoe, and already a large sum of money has been set aside for the building of a ski lift there." He urged the District Council to do all they could to see that those who were benefiting locally from skiers were aroused to take action to see that visitors to the district were encouraged in every way. He pointed out that the C.C.P.R. would be bringing in more skiers in 1955 than ever before, and that the first step towards setting up proper facilities for winter sports in the Cairngorms would be to cut down the walking time to and from the hills. He suggested that the way to do this was to extend the Glenmore road as far as the deer fence. The Badenoch District Council responded by sending their chairman, Captain Desmond Thompson, the County Clerk and the District Road Surveyor, to inspect the proposed route, along with a Forestry Commission guide. Their reply was encouraging: "We feel we should let you know that our committee, whilst very sympathetic with the proposal, have no funds at their disposal for such a project. However, we hope the matter will be considered by other interested parties, and we agree to make the initial move."

There was nevertheless a long row to hoe. Over a year later, Jock Kerr Hunter was still pointing out that although since the war, the number of skiers coming to the Cairngorms had been increased by the development of ski clubs, and the efforts of the C.C.P.R., the snowball that could grow bigger, provided proper facilities were made available, was in fact, melting away, because of the four mile "trachle up the glen". Sometimes the column was over 200 yards long as the skiers struggled, Indian file, along the two mile track. Many were exhausted before they reached the snow and obviously about a third would become so discouraged as never to return. As Kerr Hunter insisted, easy access to the snow was the foremost need in the district and any improvement would cut out a tremendous amount of drudgery.

Fortunately a couple with an enthusiasm for winter sports equal to that of Jock Kerr Hunter had recently arrived in the valley. Only a year earlier Eileen Knolles had left her job in London to take a course in overseas trade in Vienna. Her father, a former R.A.F. pilot worked for the Erna Low travel organisation and was often in Austria. She joined him one week end at a small resort. It happened to coincide with the local police ski championships. Her eye was caught by the winner, Karl Fuchs. He was the local policemen, a rather dreary job after an exciting war, when he had fought on the Russian front. There his adventures had included capturing five thousand Mongolians in long fur clothes. They had no skis, whereas the German army was well equipped for winter warfare with the exception of their uniform, which was ordinary summer issue, and had to be reinforced by layers of newspaper, worn under their vests, in an effort to retain heat against the bitter cold.

Karl was an athlete, more renowned as a runner than a skier. He trained constantly. "I never walked along the pavement," remembers Karl, "but always ran round parked cars treating them like slalom poles." Eileen and Karl were married in June of 1954. They wanted to settle quickly where they could live and work together, and imagined a future built round a small pension. Karl found that he could receive a "golden handshake" from the Austrian police, which would enable him to buy a small property. Mr. Knolles, Eileen's father, agreed to put some money into a project related to the travel business, but with the Russians so close, he was reluctant to sink this into Austria. He urged the newly married couple to come to Britain and look around for a suitable small hotel.

Accepting Mr. Knolles' advice, they wandered round the Lake District and other English areas but Karl was not enthusiastic. Then they came north, and he immediately fell in love with Scotland. "The mountain people, they were just like at home." Killin seemed the obvious place, with some of the Scottish Ski Club still gathering there during the winter months. A small hotel was for sale, but just before the decision was made, Karl travelled farther north, and caught sight of a small triangle of snow in Coire Cas. A guest house in Carrbridge was on the market, and without further thought, the decision was made. He returned to Austria and bought thirty pairs of skis with Marker cable bindings, and was back in Scotland to start the first professional commercial ski school at Struan House, Carrbridge, for the winter of 1955.

Karl and Eileen were new to the hotel trade, but with his policeman's ability to deal with catastrophes, and her capability, they soon had things under control. The first proper clients were the Navy, soon to be followed by Kurt Hahn's boys from Gordonstoun. Karl took them in his shooting-brake to wherever there was snow, moving between the

Karl Fuchs tries out the new rope tow, watched by the manufacturers reps. Jean's hut can be seen at its original site in Coire Cas.
(Cairngorm Winter Sports Development Board)

Findhorn valley and the Slochd or sometimes to behind Aviemore or over the hills to the Lecht. His pupils remember great days of fun, brought about by Karl's enthusiasm and spontaneity. He was also a perfectionist, and really did try to teach his pupils to ski.

Karl had an uncanny eye for snow; he found it on a variety of slopes, suitable for all kinds of skiers on hillsides, fields and even the golf course. The first staff that Karl took on was Plum Worrall from Manchester, who had stayed on in Scotland after a summer holiday. He was always accompanied by a small dog who was carried in his rucksack when the snow was deep. By the second season Struan House was bursting at its seams. It was an excellent winter and Karl had his hands full, as, not only had Eileen broken a leg, but their first baby, Peter, had arrived as well. Karl's infectious confidence overcame both these problems and his own lack of English, and resulted in group after group of keen, promising skiers leaving his hotel after a week's holiday.

The Fuchs soon found that they were not alone in their vision of a ski resort in the Cairngorms. Jock Kerr Hunter and several fellow enthusiasts approached Karl for advice, realising that with his continental background, he was in a position to assess the feasability of their plans. The nucleus of this group were Major A.D. Scott of Dulnain Bridge, Colin Sutton, Hugh Ross, Alistair McIntyre, Boyd Anderson, and Donnaie McKenzie, now secretary of the Scottish Ski Club, along with the main spokesman, Jock Kerr Hunter.

On March 30th 1956, the group came together and formed themselves into Strathspey Winter Sports Development Association. The first meeting, sponsored by the Scottish Council for Physical Recreation, was held in Nethybridge Hotel. It was attended by all interested parties who were united in their resolve to raise sufficient funds to build the first priority, a road. Contributions were called for, and Mr. Knolles was immediately on his feet waving a five pound note. The vice-chairman of the Scottish Tourist Board, the Provost of Inverness, Robert Wotherspoon, accepted it as the first token of public confidence in the Association's future plans. Members of the Association were surprised to notice that Colonel Grant was at the meeting. They realised that he was the one landowner in the district not entirely enthusiastic about the idea of a ski resort on the Cairngorms. This was not surprising as access across his land would be needed for the new road. They were relieved however, when he rose to his feet and congratulated the organisers, remarking that the project was most enterprising and deserved the encouragement of the whole district. He pointed out that there were three very good reasons for welcoming the advent of winter sports and encouraging them in the area. First the people who came to enjoy the beauties of the Cairngorms were a social as well as an economic asset to the district. Second, it would fill a vacuum that at the moment existed in that they suffered from a short summer season and that anything that could be done to extend that into the winter would be a valuable development. Third, he added, that as a landowner, he did not think that winter sports would conflict with any other economic interest in the area. Before he sat down he added that he had only one reservation to make, that litter was not to be left on the hillside. Otherwise he saw no reason for curtailing the skiers' access to the hills or to restricting their freedom in any way at all.

Members of the Association were so relieved at the realisation that Colonel Grant was behind them and not in opposition, that he was immediately made Chairman. The new Chairman's first step was to enlarge the Association to cover the whole area. He was successful in persuading thirty different establishments to join together to form the Strathspey and Badenoch Hotel and Boarding House Keeper's Association. This came into being three months later, its main aim being to attract tourists and particularly to develop the area as a winter sports resort. The first target was to collect £6,000 to invest in the facilities. Colonel Grant was given £168 to survey a road.

When news of these meetings of business men in the Cairngorm area came to the ears of skiers, they were somewhat sceptical. They felt that the hotel keepers were unaware of the difficulties in front of them. Philip Rankin wished that they had General Wade to advise them and felt that St. Moritz would be safe for a while from strong competition in Scotland. The skiers were comparing the Cairngorm situation with their own experience elsewhere, when a handful of club enthusiasts had both invented and erected the tows and constructed access tracks on a shoe string budget.

In the Cairngorms however, the situation was quite different. Badenoch District Council now asked their parent body, Inverness County Council to help build the new road. To everyone's surprise the Council agreed, provided the existing private road from Coylumbridge to Glenmore, which passed through Colonel Grant's land, was taken over as a county road. This could not happen until it had been brought up to the accepted Government standard at an estimated cost of £15,136.

The original group gathered together under the auspices of Jock Kerr Hunter, had now been formed into the Cairngorm Winter Sports Development Board. At their first meeting, Sir Francis Walker then Convener of the County Council, was able to tell the Board that a start was to be made on the road on March 31st and that it was to be completed within twelve months. Members were glad to hear that only a small contribution would be required from local ratepayers and that after Government grants and other donations only £3,302 out of a total cost of £36,324 need be raised from the District. Sir Francis reminded local hoteliers that they had promised £5,000 towards the scheme. He also informed them that it was the Secretary of State for Scotland, The Rt. Hon. J.S. Maclay, a keen skier and member of the Scottish Ski Club, who had decided that the money should be used for the road and not on other projects more beneficial to crofter counties in general. Colonel Grant rose to his feet to point out that this was the first occasion in which the Government, local authorities and private enterprise had come together, a new idea that he felt would be of great value to the Highland economy.

With the cost of the road off their hands, the C.W.S.D.B., as the Board was now termed, could spend the money that they had raised on lifts. After many meetings in Colonel Grant's house in Rothiemurchus, they decided that the first priority was a chairlift in the upper part of Coire Cas to run from Jean's hut to the summit ridge. It is interesting to note that another small group of engineers and businessmen, under the enthusiastic Glencoe based Jimmy Hamilton had the same idea in mind and only dropped their plans when they realised the likely success of the larger body. Instead of competing, Mr. Hamilton now joined the Board along with a key member of the Scottish Ski Club, Jim Currie.

At Easter 1960, Jim Currie walked up the rough bulldozer cut of the new road. Along with the swarms of skiers surrounding him, he found the walk to the snow greatly eased by the unfinished road. The construction work had left a scar on the face of the mountain but as he pointed out at the time, "this is a temporary disfigurement and I rejoice at the prospect of Cairngorm summit being an easy hour's climb from the car park and much less on completion of the projected chair lift." Some skiers were even lucky enough to be driven up the road precariously perched on the road builder's lorry.

By July, the road was open to motorists, but before skiers had a chance to try it out, disaster struck. On the night of August 5th, a flash flood swept away the road on either side of the new bridge across the Allt Mor. Further up the hill serious erosion occurred after the culverts were blocked by boulder debris. Undaunted the Inverness County Council immediately sent out their engineers to prepare plans and estimates for repairs. They decided that £8,000 would be needed; this was forthcoming, and the road was duly opened for the start of the next ski season.

Although the road was now open, the flood had caused the postponement of the construction of the chairlift. The summer of 1960

Opposite. Plans for the opening of the Cairngorm chairlift were put back a year when a flash flood washed out the new ski road.
(J.A. McCook)

had in fact been an unlucky period for the C.W.S.D.B. In the spring, it had placed a contract for a chair lift with a combination of Swiss and Scottish firms. The Scottish side, however, could not cope with the logistics which led to contractual difficulties, culminating in a court action, and it soon became clear that for another winter, skiers would have to rely on Bill Blackwood's efforts for uplift on the snow.

The Board was not helped by the fact that skiers themselves were often more critical than helpful, and were decidedly slow to contribute to the Board's appeal for funds. As R.O.M. Williams pointed out at the time, "Had it not been for the County Council's enlightened decision to build the Cairngorms road, there can be little doubt that Cairngorm would have remained in that natural wild state which some diehard mountain lovers still desire." The C.W.S.D.B. had a strong ally in the Forestry Commission. Not only had the Commission contributed to the cost of the road so as to improve access to its plantations but it was also enthusiastic about the proposed development which fell entirely within its boundary. There seemed to be little enthusiasm elsewhere however for the Board's proposals. The results of the public appeal had not produced nearly enough money for the plans to be put into operation. Then suddenly the situation changed. An anonymous donor offered £20,000. His only condition being that the chairlift should be a two-seater. No sooner had the press reported this, than another anonymous donor, now known to be Boyd Anderson, came forward with money for a shelter to be built at the base of the chairlift. This was to be called the "Shieling" and was to be administered by its own trustees which were to include the Scottish Ski Club's President.

Boyd Anderson was a wealthy rubber merchant who had spent his working life in the Far East. Now retired, he lived in Lossiemouth. He was 52 when he first learnt to ski, but his enthusiasm was immediate and he resolved to pass on his exhilaration and enjoyment to as many people as possible, particularly the young. When he heard that the first priority of the C.W.S.D.B. was to construct a tow he saw to it that the shelter would be constructed in parallel. The need for the Board's plans to be put into effect quickly was evident at Easter. In spite of very sparse snow at least 2,000 people crowded round Bill Blackwood's two tows. Large numbers of ski school classes occupied small pockets of snow on either side.

A fresh contract for the chairlift was negotiated with another Scottish firm and the original Swiss manufacturer provided the technical equipment and assistance for the erection of the lift itself. As the foundations for the stations and towers were prepared and the main engine and equipment collected, the Board realised that they needed an

Opposite. Bob Clyde and his new assistant Tommy Paul look over the engine of the new tow constructed by J.H. Fenner of Hull. (Cairngorm Winter Sports Development Board)

experienced manager. An advertisement was placed in the *Inverness Courier* and it was answered by Bob Clyde. At that time Bob was working as an assistant to the chief draughtsman of an engineering firm in Inverness. Weekends were spent with his Creag Dhu friends in Glencoe where he was a member of the working party running the tow. They were becoming increasingly frustrated however by the breakdown of equipment on Meall a' Bhuiridh. Instead of skiing, their free time was occupied with mending the grips on the towbar. Bob Clyde remembers that: "I answered the advertisement out of curiosity, but after discussions with my climbing friend Jimmy Hamilton, who was on the technical team for the C.W.S.D.B., I became more interested. I was interviewed by Major Scott, and his enthusiasm for the scheme took a hold of me and I decided I wanted the job."

Major Scott realised that here was the ideal man for their project. Bob was appointed and on his suggestion, the control of the job of erecting the chairlift was taken from the contractors, and put entirely in his hands. Needing staff, he immediately looked to the Creag Dhu. The necessary qualifications of being able to climb ice-encased pylons in a winter blizzard, and then carry out an engineering job, called for skills particularly suited to "hard climbers". One of the Creag Dhu, recently returned from New Zealand, was Tommy Paul. He decided that the idea of working in the hills on a full time basis was attractive, and answered Bob's invitation with alacrity.

Bob's enthusiasm and his carefully selected team enabled the chairlift to be officially opened on December 23rd 1961, at a cost of £42,000. The Shieling, complete with plumbing, and its own electricity, was in use by the following season. While the C.W.S.D.B. was obviously a commercial concern, it operated for one purpose only, to provide facilities for the skiers in the Cairngorms area.

The Board now had to decide what to charge for the use of the new lift. They had to strike a balance between what skiers could afford and what the Board needed to pay off loans, remunerate staff, maintain and insure the lift as well as build up a reserve for further development. With this in mind it was decided to make a basic charge for the winter season of 1961, of 4 shillings per trip on the lift, whether up or down, and a reduction for quantity by the sale of books of eight tickets for £1, or forty trips for £4. Ski clubs and local hotels who had supported the project, were to be given a special rate, and also, the opportunity to buy a limited number of season tickets. As was stressed at the time, the Board was to be a non-profit distributing body and as result, any surplus funds, after meeting necessary outgoings, were to be used for further developments of the skiing facilities in the area. Already there were plans for the erection of a trainer-type ski tow, in Coire Cas, and a longer one in the easterly Coire na Ciste.

The day of the rope tow was now over in the Cairngorms. One skier remembered regretfully that: "Those were the days – the sensual feel of the rope slurping through the wet gloves, the pain complex as one's arms were tortured, giving way to a feeling of elation and relief at finally making it to the top." No more amateur tow operators, armed with broken spanners, bent nails and a hammer, for now Bob Clyde and Tommy Paul had been joined by other members of the Creag Dhu: Bill Smith and Harry McKay. The first British members of a new elite profession, winter sports engineers.

Harry McKay, left, and Tommy Paul, right, were members of the climbing elite in Glencoe before coming to work for the Cairngorm Winter Sports Development Board on Cairngorm. (M.R. Kenneth)

9. Ski Schools & Clubs

Karl Fuchs had been the first continental to have confidence in Scotland
as a place to ski. He had been so encouraged by the potential of his school
after the first few years, that he asked the immigration authorities for
permits to bring in five young trainers from the Arlberg area of Austria
to staff his classes. He was in fact allowed only one permit, and this was
taken up by a young skier from his own village, Hans Kuwall.

After a successful season Hans married Barbara, a housekeeper at
Struan House, and the young couple moved to found another ski school
at the Carrbridge Hotel. There were plenty of clients, however, for two
establishments. Some 2,000 people had now learned to ski under Karl's
instruction. With this increase in numbers and an improvement in
standards Karl felt that ski races should now be held on Cairngorm. He
set a course down Coire na Ciste with the 48 gates laid out in the same
pattern as the 1948 Olympic event at St Moritz.

Karl's activities in Scotland drew the attention of other continentals to
the area. The Norwegian Tourist Board wanted to link their name with
winter sports in Scotland and backed the "Scotland/Norway Ski
School" that was set up at Grantown-on-Spey. This was at the
suggestion of Colonel Sandvik, who thought that the Scots should adopt
the Norwegian method of instruction, and also cement the friendship
forged during the war. There was also the "Scottish-Swiss School of
skiing" whose headquarters were at the Nethybridge Hotel. Here, at a
charge of 13 guineas, pupils could have a week's instruction with
transport to the hills and entertainment in the evenings.

Karl's footsteps had also been followed by Michelle Bochatay from
Champery, who set up his ski school in Deeside. His main contribution
to Scottish skiing was an emphasis on Swiss precision. Even in the
pouring rain he always looked immaculate. Despite muddy conditions he
left the hill as spruce as when he stepped out of his landrover in the
morning. Unassuming and shy, any witty remark he did make was in
broad Buchan. The greatest praise he was ever heard to give to any of his
damp, dishevelled, dirty pupils was "Eet was net bad". Aberdeen skiers

seeking his instruction would look for a large orange flag placed in the snow. Here for the first time in Britain they could take the official tests of the Swiss Ski School.

There were students from the continent as well as instructors skiing in Scotland and in 1961 Norwegians made a clean sweep of all the main trophies. Frith Finlayson was one of those to become indignant with the number of Norwegian names on the cups. He felt especially that among the instructors there was no need for foreign accents on the hill. He stated that "If we are going to sell Scotland as a ski country in its entirety, the bulk of teachers must be Scottish." He also felt it was nonsense for such a proliferation of ski styles, maintaining that the basic movements of good skiing were identical.

Frith knew that he had to perfect his own style if people were going to accept his opinion. He could not possibly beat the foreign instructors without becoming one of them. With this in mind he travelled to Lauterbrunnen, Switzerland, engaged Werner Steiger as an instructor and soon became his personal friend. Werner had never met anyone quite like Frith. His fantastic energy and fitness were in direct contrast to that of the usual British Alpine skier. Werner was expected to join him on the first uplift in the morning and continue to ski all day till the last chair down. The language barrier was not a problem, "except oan the dance flair, you never knew if she wis giving you the patter or shoutin' fir the polis." Frith was taken aback by the crowds, waiting for the cog-railway but "we soon got the hang of it and shouted, 'Ootzen den Roaden!' in shrill voices, and they just melted away, leaving us a clear road onto the first carriage."

Frith made yearly excursions to the Swiss Ski School instructors's course, and this ultimately led him to receive the prized Ski School Director's Certificate in 1961. It was said of him at the time that "Frith is the most polished, indigenous skier in Britain today. There may be faster racers, but few can cope so expertly with any type of snow, and this is the real test."

Having perfected his own technique, Frith made sure that his instructors raised their standards to match his. Realising that they could not all travel out to Switzerland to qualify as Swiss instructors, the alternative was to set up the same type of establishment at home. With this in mind, he was the prime mover in the creation of the British Association of Professional Ski Instructors, and in the spring of 1961, he set up the first qualifying course, admonishing and encouraging the participants with his sharp Clydeside tongue. Clean boots and pressed trousers were as important as parallel Christies. The foreign instructors in Scotland were hostile, and even scornful of Frith's attempts and many

Frith Finlayson "the most polished indigenous skier in Britain" he was the prime mover in the formation of the British Association of Professional Ski Instructors.
(Robert Benzies)

Scottish skiers seemed to prefer to be told to "Bend se knees" in a broken accent than be shouted at by Frith. However, by setting a high standard, Frith improved the teaching of all the ski schools in Britain, as the continentals realised that they could no longer get away with little skiing ability and slap-happy instruction. Most had come to Britain to learn to speak English and had found that ski teaching was a useful means to that end.

Ski development in Scotland, though, seemed to take two steps forward to one back. It was a sad blow to Scottish skiers when the Spittal Hotel, the home of the Dundee Ski Club was burnt to the ground. Major improvements in Glenshee were nevertheless underway. The club, under the supervision of David Jamieson, had embarked on a five year plan to build two tows and suitable huts to serve both areas. Due to great efforts by club members the work was completed on schedule. It was a very different picture to that in the Cairngorms:

"A skier once told us, I hope he never lied
That he knew a slope on a far hillside.
Where, in the winter, there was bags of snow,
And so we decided to build a tow.

We carried up pylons, we carried up logs,
Over ruddy rocks, and through blooming bogs,
We carried up iron, bolts and steel
And then carried up a ruddy great wheel.

We blistered each hand and blistered each heel,
Our language even blistered the lumps of steel,
We put up miles of fencing to make the snow
Drift around the pylons we built in a row.

We put up a hut on top and put inside
That tractor which we dragged up that far hillside,
The hut was to shield the tractor from the snow,
And the tractor was there to drive the ruddy tow.

Simpson, M.B., was driver of our jeep,
He always bogged it axle deep,
Due to this he is so famed,
That 'that bogger, Simpson' he is now named.

Then we came to the better bit,
Arrived in time for testing it,
The engineer, full of doubts and fears,
Started up his engine and crashed in his gears.

Then round and round went the shaft of steel,
And round and round went the ruddy great wheel,

A bald headed eagle went higher and higher,
Running up the up track hanging on the wire.

Back in the bar the champagne flowed,
Back in the bar, our faces glowed,
We knew all we needed now was snow,
To repay us for the time spent building our tow.

The strength of a ski club comes from those family members, who are prepared to spend time and effort on projects for the next generation of skiers. Such were the Jamiesons. David now had three daughters, who, owing to his dedication, were creeping up the race result lists. One wet Sunday, the youngest was heard to moan, "Daddy, it's cold. I want to go home." "Don't be silly darling," was his reply, "It's not dark yet."

Glenshee was becoming more and more popular due to its ski tows being the most accessible in Scotland. The Dundee Ski Club, the nucleus of this activity, was growing fast, with its membership rising each year. Skiers in Scotland wanted to be where the action was. The fact that Sheila Jamieson, though still a junior, was the fastest lady in Scotland, had been noticed, and other skiers felt that by coming to the same area their own standard would be raised.

The hub of the activity in Glenshee was a group of exuberant, good skiers: Ian Steven; David Banks; Jack Duncan; David Farquharson; David Anderson and Bob Benzies. This was quite a separate group to that found on Meall a' Bhuiridh, the skiers only coming together at race meetings. The Tennant Trophy was the event that drew most skiers to Glenshee, and was by far the most popular race on the calendar. To use the tows in Glenshee skiers had to be members of either the Dundee or the Scottish Ski Club. More people were however coming into the area, and there was pressure on the organisers to change the regulations. While each club had a nucleus of people who believed that the tows should be retained in club hands, others were more far-sighted. They thought that they should off-load their responsibilities to a commercial enterprise. This would allow the clubs to return to the fun of skiing and not be continually concerned with maintenance problems and the selling of tickets.

Aberdeen skiers liked to ski in Glenshee but by January the roads to the Devil's Elbow were usually blocked and Braemar was the limit of their skiing expeditions. To overcome the problem they founded the Aberdeen Ski Club, specifically to provide accessible uplift facilities. By the enterprise of Hylas Holbourn, a tractor was procured and converted into a mobile tow. It was driven to Abergeldie, some six miles beyond Ballater, and set up at the top of a field, adjacent to the main Deeside

123

Road. Skiing here could last five or six weeks, and in good weather, was said to equal conditions in Glenshee. Members hung on to a rope driven by the tractor and were hauled up to the top of Geallaig Hill. The tow was 300 yards long, and gave six hundred skiers per hour a vertical lift of about 450 feet. Hylas Holbourn warned members of the club that this was a "powerful and dangerous toy". He told them to guard against over-enthusiasm, as this might cause the tractor providing the motive power, to hurtle down the slope, mowing down everyone in its path.

The fields at Abergeldie soon became so congested that a letter appeared in the press from a beginner who said he had been terrified by the "downhill boys" tearing through the middle of the field, and asked if it was possible for the police to institute some form of control over the slopes. The editor calmly pointed out that this was an international problem, and that the Braemar police had had no new skis issued to them since the Scottish Ski Club had presented a pair in 1907. He suggested that the only solution was to hurl abuse at the maniac, to warn other skiers of the menace in their midst and, at the first opportunity to break his skis over his head.

Later, the tractor was moved to the Lecht, on land belonging to the Forbes family. Members of the Aberdeen Club could also use the Scottish Ski Club's portable tow now permanently fixed on Carn-an-Tuirc. The two clubs erected a commodious wooden hut, one and a half miles up the hill, a good hour's walk from the road. In the Aberdeen Ski Club's first handbook, it was pointed out that "this was done for your special benefit, so that you may shelter inside, rubbing sodden shoulders with what seems like the full membership of both clubs, looking out through the storm-proof windows, bulging under the pent-up fury of the Arctic blizzards, which is the choicest feature of this locale."

The Aberdeen Ski Club also organised a dry ski school, in the premises of the Rubber Shop, in George Street. For one shilling members could practise exercises and walk about on hired skis, thus becoming familiar with the equipment and to make the most out of their day on the hill. Membership of the club was ten shillings and for a further fifteen shillings, members could hire skis, sticks and boots for the day. The bus cost ten shillings, with coffee and biscuits thrown in. This bus generally headed for the Devil's Elbow, some 68 miles from Aberdeen, stopping en route at the Sheann Spittal bridge from where members could walk across to their hut on Carn-an-Tuirc.

It is interesting to note that while both the first president of the Scottish Ski Club, William Spiers Bruce, and the original Dundee Ski Club pioneer, Colonel Butchart, had both come from Aberdeen, it was only now, that the city formed a club of its own. It was the Aberdeen Ski

Opposite. With the road blocked at the Devil's Elbow, Glenshee skiers had to make do with fields further down the glen.
(Robert Benzies Album)

Club however who were to organise the first cross country race in Scotland. It was held on February 14th 1960. The course was set half way up the Geallaig Hill and took a zig-zag route down to the gate of a field, then through two more to the finish at the road. The competitors and organisers had to walk through waist deep soft snow drifts to reach the start. As it was to be a geschmozzle start, all competitors had to wait while one struggled to pull on his frozen gloves. At last the whistle blew, but then it was found that the delay had resulted in several skiers becoming frozen to the spot and they wasted seconds before getting on their way. The first person to fall, disappeared completely and then re-appeared a few yards further down the course. On reaching the small uphill section, the racers found that it was a sheet of solid ice, covered with a thin layer of snow. After this came the tricky run down through the woods. There was great excitement when the first two snow-covered competitors crossed the finishing line, within fractions of a second of each other.

Other areas of Scotland were also being patronised by skiers. The Lowther Hills, South of Glasgow, rise to 2,400 feet, with long grass covered ridges and six intervening north facing gullies, lying between the two highest tops of Green Lowther and Lowther Hill. Alistair Borthwick of the B.B.C. visited the area in 1952, to record local colour for his programme "Country Magazine". This had resulted in publicity for the Lowthers as a ski area and enthusiasts from Dumfries came together, to form the South of Scotland Ski Club in 1953. The club's headquarters were the Hopetown Arms Hotel, Leadhills, Lanarkshire. John Hilton was the Manager and with his enthusiasm, the club grew from strength to strength and procured a small tow which was first operated in the season of 1956. The South of Scotland Ski Club obtained permission to use the private road to the radar station on the summit of Lowther Hill. With a bus to the top of the run, the club became popular, particularly with U.S. airmen stationed at Prestwick.

Northern skiers were also active. A bus left Inverness every Sunday morning heading for Garve, 28 miles away. The Garve Hotel, run by Miss McKenzie, was the centre for the Highland Ski Club, numbering about 700 in the late 1950s. This club had originally consisted of members of the Lovat Scouts who formed it at their first post-war reunion. They had trained in winter in both Canada and Iceland, and were anxious to carry on skiing as a pastime after the war. Their favourite skiing ground was the western slope of Ben Wyvis. This was reached from near Garbat, in the Valley of the Black Water, about six miles from Garve. A climb of over 1,000 feet was usually necessary before skiing could be attempted. The four main snow holding gullies are protected from the full force of the mild prevailing south-west wind, by the mountains to the west. Two of the gullies face north of west, and the other two face south of west, thus giving varying snow conditions. The Highland Ski Club had plans for erecting a hut and a tow there but these never came to anything.

While local clubs flourished, the national club, the Scottish Ski Club had its problems. Many of its members resented the amount of club funds and energy that were tied into Glencoe, which they could not readily reach at the weekend. After all the efforts to construct the ski tow, Meall a' Bhuiridh was now out of favour. Enthusiasm for skiing in Glencoe had been falling. For three seasons the snow had been disappointing in the west. Freezing thick cloud accompanied by high wind made skiing conditions miserable and the operation of the tow difficult. What snow there was had been turned into ice and as Easter approached very few people were prepared to ski down the glazed, canted, corniced chute that led to the bottom of the tow lift. Once there it was extemely difficult to gain uplift via the tow itself as ice had formed in the inside of the grips.

The season ended with loans of £2,850 still to be paid off including £900 from the Scottish Ski Club's central fund. A further £1,000 was needed to pay the final instalment of the British Ropeway Engineering Company's bill. It was felt that the main deterrent to skiing on Meall a' Bhuiridh was the steep walk up to the foot of the tow, and this could be overcome by the construction of a chairlift. The management committee of the Scottish Ski Club however had other priorities. They considered that the building of a hut there to be of far more importance to their members than a chairlift. They also felt that if the club was going to put in more uplift it should be on a completely different site. Philip Rankin countered by pointing out that if the club was really going to erect a lift elsewhere, a totally new work party crew would be needed, and there were just not enough people with the available knowledge. He urged the club to back his plan. "Now, dependent only on you is a lift project which just a few years ago you would likely have called a crazy pipe-dream. Within twelve months of reading about it, you can ride on it, if you say so. You can believe or not, as you choose, the prophecy attached that, before many years are out, it will break the doldrums of the far north and turn Scottish skiing from a weekend ploy for some hundreds, into a holiday sport for thousands."

Philip's enthusiasm once again stirred the members of the Scottish Ski Club. They authorised the committee to proceed with the construction of the proposed chair-lift, provided a sum of £4,000 could be raised from members. The meeting had no sooner adjourned than a message was

received that the sum of £20,000 had been deposited in trust for the development of skiing in the Cairngorms. Bearing in mind that the objective of the Scottish Ski Club was to provide facilities for and the promotion of, skiing in the whole of Scotland, the management committee felt that the Cairngorms Winter Sports Development Board had to be supported. They put forward the motion that all contributions so far collected for the Glencoe chairlift should be transferred to the Cairngorms. After much discussion it was agreed that the Glencoe project should be abandoned. Philip Rankin remarked at the time that "our little sprat of an idea was chased off the water by this splendid shining new bait, to be erected in the Cairngorms". He realised that private enterprise was needed. With this in mind, he approached the landowner, Major Fleming and asked him to consider financing the full development on Meall a' Bhuiridh. To Philip Rankin's surprise he agreed to spend the sum of £12,000, provided the club handed over the Glencoe tow complete with its equipment, and its rights to tenancy.

The club hastily organised a special general meeting. Members who had put a great deal of effort into the Glencoe project, were furious and indignant at the thought of the club off-loading the tow, now that it was capable of making a profit. But the issue put before the meeting at Stirling was quite simple, the tow needed a substantial injection of money, and none of those dissenting had a credible suggestion as to where this could come from. Philip had a positive alternative which would certainly result in uplift being available in Glencoe for the next season. It was against this background that a vote was taken and it was unanimously agreed that the tow should be handed over to the landowner. The conditions were that he carried out the full development and paid the club the sum of £500 which would then be used to build a shelter on the hill. Philip Rankin remembers that at the time he was not quite sure whether this decision "represented a failure of a mission, or a sterling success". There is no doubt that the Scottish Ski Club showed tremendous enterprise in setting up the first overhead rope tow in Scotland. In handing it over now, they lost some of their most vigorous members, but ski tow operations had become too big for the amateur.

Skiing in Glencoe was to be run by a private company, under the name of "White Corries", with Major Fleming and Philip Rankin as directors. The nucleus of the work party transferred their allegiance to the new company. By the end of the summer of 1959, having moved twelve tons of concrete, two tons of steelwork, and having transferred the Lister engine to a new site they were able to say that the new T-bar ski tow would be in operation for the new season, designed to carry four hundred passengers per hour.

Opposite. The Geschmozzle start of the first cross country race held by the Aberdeen Ski Club on the Geallaig Hill, February 1960.
(Press and Journal)

The rover scouts mountain rescue team
at Glenshee. Casualties were asked to
make a donation to scout funds.
(Robert Benzies Collection)

The plastic slope at Hillend, on the
outskirts of Edinburgh, is the largest in
Europe.
(M.R. Kenneth)

10. INNOVATION

By the early sixties more and more people were skiing in Scotland each year. No longer were they all clad in ex-army waterproofs. Colours were appearing on the hills. Trousers termed "vorlage" tapered in at the boot.

Release bindings of various types were now in general use. In spite of these new bindings, accidents were becoming more frequent. This was blamed on the fact that skiers were not now as fit as they used to be when forced to walk uphill. In Glencoe a ski patrol service was run by what had been the "Wee Yins". The official rescue service in Glenshee was run by the Boy Scouts. They wore yellow armbands whilst on duty, and spent the night at the Glenshee Schoolhouse. To raise the necessary money to run the scheme casualties were asked to donate to Scout Funds.

Through the years, victims were full of praise for the Scouts, particularly, when they adopted "jet splints". This was a development consisting of twin layers of plastic in the shape of the leg or arm which when placed over an injury could be blown up quickly to clamp the broken limb firmly between layers of compressed air, thus providing warmth and support. The splints were made by the Mine Safety Appliances Ltd., of Shettleston, Glasgow, and were presented to the team by the Harp Lager Company. The Chief Scout himself, Sir Charles MacLean, came to Glenshee to watch members of the Rover crew carry out a mock rescue operation. He also presented a medal to one of the team, who had run eight miles for help, when an avalanche overtook three companions in the Cairngorms. Two had died, but the other was found alive, twenty two hours later. It was due to this publicity that the Murphy Radio Company installed about £1,000 worth of radio telephone equipment to be used for communications with the ambulance network.

Many of the new skiers were children who had been introduced to the sport by the education authorities. The Dundee and Scottish Ski Clubs jointly sponsored the first schools race on February 11th 1962. It was run in a gully near the Meall Odhar tow. Conditions were so atrocious that had it been a club race, the event would have been cancelled, but since the organising of thirty five assorted boys and girls onto one piece of snow was difficult to repeat, the organisers carried on. The idea behind the race was to encourage local schools to become involved in the skiing scene, as in the Alps, where the best junior racers came from the high villages. In the event, it was only Blairgowrie High School that could be said to be local. Morrison's Academy was first, Glenalmond second, and Strathallan third.

In 1962 junior racers were offered another incentive. Hamish Liddell persuaded Nestlé's to present three scholarships of £100 each to be administered by the Scottish Ski Club. The money was to be spent by the winners for training abroad and the Kandahar Ski Club agreed to accept the three lucky children into their training scheme. Hamish Liddell said at the time that "This scheme is a direct encouragement to the young skier. No really outstanding youngster is now denied the chance of going abroad for lack of finance. It is hoped that this is a beginning and in the not too distant future young Scottish racers will be knocking on the door of the British Team." Hamish Liddell and his friend Lewis Drysdale were intent on raising the standard of racing in Scotland by bringing about a more sophisticated and professional attitude to its organisation. They felt that racing improved the standard of all skiers. They persuaded the club to invest in electronic timing equipment so that never again could competitors complain, as one had, to the editor of the Ski Club Journal in 1953:

> "Dear Sir,
> I wish to protest of the very slack arrangements which were made for the race run on Meall a' Bhuiridh on 26th April.
> I was duly started off at the top as number 39 by a timekeeper with a watch. When I reached the finish I found the timekeeper had gone home. Is this sportsman-like?
> I am, Sir, your obedient servant,
> R.R. Taylor."

Electronic timing was first used in the Scottish Kandahar of 1962. The course setter's equipment on this occasion also included crampons, steel bar and mallet.

Skiers were not only competing on snow. A plastic material had been developed for the construction of artificial ski slopes. Many had dreamt of finding a substitute to snow for use during the summer months and everything from sand to pine needles had been tried. The first practical answer, was the idea of the Italian Acquaderni, who had invented rush matting. It was similar to the bristles of a brush pointing upwards, held by a lattice-like pattern of metal strips formed into mats a yard wide and about two long. These could be laid on a wooden slope indoors or outside on a steep hillside to form a slalom course.

Plastic snow's first appearance in England was due to the enterprise of Simpson's of Piccadilly who set up a slope behind Earl's Court. The new plastic mat came into its own at the 1962 International Winter Sports Exhibition in London. There were about thirty stands, taken by equipment manufacturers and importers, as well as travel agents, and national tourist boards, but the main attraction in the grand hall was the 50 foot high, 200 foot long indoor ski run. It had a run out onto coconut matting surrounded by a barricade of jute bags filled with sawdust. A single bar ski tow ran alongside, and for 7/6d the public could have the use of this slope for 20 minutes.

The grand opening ceremony was performed by the reigning world champion Karl Schranz. The Scots were represented by a demonstration team from Glenshee, reinforced by Rudi Prochazka of Badenoch. Races were held on the slope every night, set by a joiner who drilled holes in the wood in which flags were placed. Prizes of holidays in the Alps as well as Glenshee and the Cairngorms were awarded.

The event was repeated the following year with a race between professional instructors from Scotland and England. The team from the north was made up of: Rudy Prochazka, Frith Finlayson, Ludwig Langreiter, Karl Fuchs and Hans Kuwall. Hans remembers that after the race a large man invited him for a drink. Over a half pint of lager and a Woodbine he asked Hans's opinion of the plastic matting. Hans had enjoyed his evening's skiing and had been more successful than the other members of his team, so he spoke enthusiastically in its favour.

The large man was Boyd Anderson, just waiting for an enthusiast to back his plan for the erection of a plastic slope of some magnitude on the Pentland Hills outside Edinburgh. He invited Hans to help him put the idea into operation. Boyd Anderson had moved from Lossiemouth to Edinburgh in 1957. With the Pentland Hills on his doorstep he began to wonder how he could lengthen their skiing possibilities from more than a few days in the year. On a business trip to Munich he heard of the artificial snow mountain that had just been erected outside the city. He visited this and began to see the possibility of producing in Scotland a real opportunity to teach people to ski all the year round. The Scottish Council for Physical Recreation and Edinburgh Corporation greeted his plans with enthusiasm, and he erected a small experimental artificial slope at Lothianburn Golf Course. He was an active participant, spending his time on the site among the carpenters, with hammer, measuring tape and spirit level. He was constantly altering and

Boyd Anderson, left and Lewis Drysdale. It was Boyd Anderson's enthusiasm and financial backing that ed to the creation of the plastic slope at Hillend.
M.R. Kenneth)

133

improving his plans, and when any new idea appeared in the newspapers, or foreign ski journals, he followed it up at once. John Cook, Deputy Director of Education for Edinburgh Corporation at the time, remembered that: "Barytes was suggested as a possible skiing surface, so I went with him to a remote North Yorkshire lead mine, schussed down a crumbling cliff of heavy pebbles, and soon found myself with a lorry load of the stuff at the foot of the new slope at Hillend. He ensured that nothing worthwhile was missed. I never ceased to marvel at his youthful zeal, his capacity for sheer hard work, his painstaking attention to detail at all times, but most of all, his determination to achieve more and more for the benefit of others. He was the most self-effacing of men, shunning publicity of any kind and wanting only the simplest of pleasure for himself."

Out of this, of course, grew the largest plastic slope in the world. It reached its full fruition in 1965, complete with a chairlift, whose attendant wore a bus conductor's uniform, as Edinburgh Corporation had incorporated it in their normal transport facility to rate-payers. Racers felt that the plastic slope was similar to skiing on sheet ice. As one remarked: "Skiing on the plastic called for an exactness of technique – it was much less forgiving than snow, and the slightest lapse of concentration spelt disaster. This meant that it was excellent for training and of course, beginning. Scottish skiers usually have atrocious technique as they have taught themselves on a windswept, snowless, muddy patch at the bottom of a ski area."

The first race on the plastic surface was held in 1966. The course was 200 yards long, on varied slopes of Dendix matting with grass already showing green between the mesh. Hans Kuwall had set the thirty two gate slalom and the timing was carried out by yet another innovation of Boyd Anderson's, an illuminated board which flashed the passage of seconds as each competitor ran down the course. The Lord Provost of Edinburgh was there. He afterwards donated a tea, to not only the competitors, but gatekeepers and organisers as well. The race was won by Tony Wimmer, from Saalbech, in Austria. He had actually come to Britain as a tennis coach, but had contacted Hans Kuwall to ask if there were any openings for a keen skier in Britain. Hans immediately invited Tony to join him on the plastic slope, knowing that he was an Austrian B Team trainee and so would be an asset to the Hillend Artificial Slope, as it was now to be officially called.

Boyd Anderson died in 1972, and in June of that year a plaque was unveiled by his widow, dedicating the centre to the memory of the man "whose vision and generosity made everything here possible. He sought the best and when he found it, he gave it away to others to enjoy." Even

Hans Kuwall in action on the plastic.
(M.R. Kenneth)

An advanced class from the Ski Club of
Great Britain being instructed at Hillend
by Hans Kuwall.
(M.R. Kenneth)

Derek Brightman and the snow making machine installed by the Dalmunzie Hotel in Glenshee.
(Robert Benzies)

more of a memorial to Boyd Anderson's vision is the fact that 170,000 school pupils passed through the gate at Hillend in 1980, surely his dream come true.

Glenshee meanwhile was booming. A new chairlift had been erected, not by the Dundee Ski Club, as the other uplift in the area had been, but by a group from the club calling themselves the Glenshee Chairlift Company Ltd. The County Council had stepped in to improve the area with a snow fence along the road from the Devil's Elbow to the summit and by the provision of more car-parking, at a cost of £26,000. The Dalmunzie Hotel nearby had installed an artificial snow making machine. Compressed air and water were mixed at freezing temperature and shot at force out of a hose spraying fine particles of "snow" on the surface of the ground. This was all very well on the days of no wind, but otherwise the resulting mixture tended to float away into space.

By far the most ambitious project was that of the Penchaud brothers. They had bought Mar Lodge, an estate of some 60,000 acres and set about launching it as a ski resort on a size quite unprecedented in Scotland. The Lodge itself, around which everything was planned was well sheltered by huge pine trees. Among these, two ski lifts were erected, one for beginners, a T bar, with a capacity of 600 per hour, and a length of 620 feet; the other, for more experienced skiers with a capacity of 800 per hour, and a range of 2,050 feet, giving a vertical height of skiing of 600 feet. The ski slopes were specially tailored and cleared of rocks and tree roots. As the season of 1965 opened, Mar Lodge announced that "it had Europe's largest artificial snow making plant, covering an area of 20 acres, and so able to extend the skiing season by several weeks. Also there were two restaurants with bar, après ski dancing in their historic ballroom, heated changing and shower rooms, a children's crèche, first aid post, resident ski instructors, a huge car park for over 1,000 vehicles, plus full ski equipment hire service, ski lock-ups and runs to suit all standards, ranging from easy open slopes to fast, thrilling descents through the forest."

It was a magnificent idea; a bold and imaginative financial gamble, in an area known to the older skiers as having excellent potential. A five mile ski run had been reported on Beinn-a-Bhuird, lying beyond Mar Lodge, the previous year. The Penchaud brothers realised that they were out on a limb. Their estate was six miles from the nearest public road, but they felt that the potential of the slopes on Beinn-a-Bhuird were so great that their estate would act as a honeypot to all the skiers in Scotland. Their confidence had been built up by several years of heavy snow. They were to find however that Scottish weather can never be depended upon. In 1963 no natural snow fell on the area and the temperature seldom reached freezing point. In the few days when the temperature did drop it was accompanied by a strong wind which blew the artificial snow in all directions. The brothers had not expected this as the area was well sheltered by the forest which grew 300 feet higher in Mar than it did in Glenmore.

At last a windless frosty night occurred and the oldest Penchaud brother rushed to the machinery controlling the artificial snow and switched it on. To his surprise no water ran into the pump, and, on investigating the burn, he was horrified to find that it had frozen up completely. The brothers had never thought that their plans would be foiled by lack of water. As with so many commerical dreams for the Highlands the realities of the weather proved insurmountable.

As the machinery of the Penchaud brothers lay rusting in the rain, plans were being drawn up by Hugh Fraser, for an equally ambitious project on the other side of the Cairngorms, at Aviemore. Others had also decided that the Northern Cairngorms offered greatest potential for ski development in Scotland. Frith Finlayson had already moved his ski school from Glencoe to the grounds of the Cairngorm Hotel. British Rail offered reduced fare tickets to skiers travelling to Aviemore, Boat of Garten, Carrbridge, Nethybridge, Kincraig, Kingussie and Newtonmore.

Mar Lodge, a ski development that failed for lack of snow. (Scottish Ski Club Journal)

Ian Finlayson at Glencoe. He later raced
for Britain at the Sapporo Olympics.
(Finlayson Collection)

Glencoe Ski Club Lodge, built by the
members themselves.
(Scottish Ski Club Journal)

11. ENTERPRISE

The ski clubs of Scotland were involved with all branches of the sport, but at 2 a.m. on November 11th 1961, a club was born with one priority: to encourage young skiers to become familiar with racing requirements and techniques and to provide them with the necessary training and encouragement. The Glencoe Ski Club was Scotland's first purely racing club.

Enthusiasm abounded although cash was short. Membership was restricted to active participants. With great energy the small club built its own residential lodge at Bridge of Orchy. It had been constructed entirely by members. Out of a membership of 68 only 14 had not worked on the project and so they were asked to resign. Chris Lyon drew up two rules for the hut. Courtesy and commonsense, and five people were delegated to make sure that these were obeyed.

Despite new clubs springing up in various parts of the country, responsibilities for the organisation of major races still lay with the Scottish and Dundee Ski Clubs. The president of the Scottish Ski Club, Lewis Drysdale, heard however, that a new federation was to be formed in London, which would assume responsibility for all skiing affairs in Britain, at home and abroad. Drysdale was a strong nationalist and he immediately decided that the only way to outwit such a happening was to form a larger and stronger association north of the border. His first move was to organise a conference of the Scottish ski clubs. At this meeting it was agreed to form the Scottish National Ski Council, which would assume the national functions which had been carried out in the past by the Scottish Ski Club. This would leave the Club with the responsibility for the organisation of its own races, provision of huts, journals and other services for its own members. It was stated at the time, though, that the Scottish Ski Club would have a large say in the workings of the new Council and its views would always be given their due weight in any national decision. The Council was to represent Scottish interests at the proposed National Ski Federation of Great Britain, when it came into effect. The Scottish Ski Club would

Glencoe, 1979, lower chair looking up to the Scottish Ski Club Hut. (M.R. Kenneth)

nevertheless continue to represent Scottish interests on the Council of the Ski Club of Great Britain.

The eighteen clubs which formed the new Council represented 5,400 skiers. It was agreed that each skier should pay an annual subscription of 5/-d. per head, a shilling of which would be passed on to the National Federation when required. The decisions were confirmed at the first A.G.M. in May 1964, when Lewis Drysdale was elected President. The Vice President was S. Henderson of the Dundee Ski Club, while representatives from the Glencoe, Highland, Aberdeen and the Edinburgh Civil Service Ski Clubs formed the executive committee.

An organisation of this scale needed a paid secretary. Major Guy Chilver-Stainer came forward to fill the gap. Guy had been a former manager of the British Olympic Cross Country Team, secretary of the Ski Club of Great Britain, Youth Officer with the L.C.C. and Editor of various ski magazines. It was this latter occupation that had brought him to Scotland.

The Council was looked at warily by many club skiers. They were suspicious that it would emasculate the clubs and give a small group of people tremendous authority over skiing in Scotland. However, it was felt by others that it was important for the skiers to speak with one voice when dealing with F.I.S., the winter sports industry, and government-aid bodies and that if the clubs pooled their resources in the fields of training and racing, all skiers would benefit.

The first practical event held by the Scottish National Ski Council, was a course in race timing. About fifty people attended and gained experience in hand timing and photo-cell apparatus. As the course was held in early October, cars travelling along the Pitlochry road were used instead of skiers. The drivers looked surprised as large groups of people closely followed their progress, with the aid of watches, wires, lamps, instrument panels and headphones. As a result of the course racers were informed that in future their time would be recorded accurately to within one tenth of a second.

Equally important from the racing point of view, was the influence that the S.N.S.C. exerted on the National Ski Federation to come into line with other skiing nations over the F.I.S. rule on amateurism. This resulted in ski instructors being allowed to compete in the open races held in Scotland. The standard of skiing in races was immediately seen to rise and interest in competition led the S.N.S.C. to appoint a racing coach, Norbert Uitz. He realised that Scotland's hope for success in international racing lay with the juniors, so he persuaded the Council to provide money to the clubs who had junior training schemes.

The S.N.S.C. also made their presence felt in the organisation of

The start of a race before electronic
timing.
(Mackenzie Album)

"Dead Man's Gulch" Glencoe, Scottish
Kandahar 1956.
(Mackenzie Album)

major races such as the Pitman Quaich of 1964. This was held in the upper basin of Meall a' Bhuiridh, down which Hans Kuwall set a course of 39 gates on what was known as "Glencoe Ice". It was a day for "stottin aff ra granite". Competitors were said to have been so surprised when they came across a patch of real snow, that they stopped to make closer acquaintance. One remembers that: "Hans had been pretty chirpy doing his course setting, but he became distinctly alarmed when he learned that he had to vorlauf his creation as well. By now, the sun had come out to relieve a cold wind, and the racers were nervously gibbering as they gathered their numbers at the start. The starters in their plastic tent opened their bottle and all was ready – off went Hans, through the first five gates, over a bumpy shoulder, into a icy hairpin. At that point he disappeared into the rocks. The lesser mortals watching their supposed betters performing, began to realise that mere survival would inevitably mean a good placing. Remarks like 'I'm going slowly' and 'Gees-oh! If they canna do it...' George Bruce decided that there was nothing to lose, not even his own ski, for he used his sister's, and his fine attacking, controlled runs made him an easy winner. The only other approach to his speed was Ian Steven. There was an exciting flush towards the end of the course, which he succeeding in taking straight. Unfortunately, this also meant taking away part of the timing equipment at the finish. The unflappability of the time-keepers was worth watching."

A major influence in the Scottish racing scene had been the annual competition between the Norwegians. Reciprocal visits had been maintained for ten years. The Norwegians looked upon this as a great event, particularly when the Scots, financed by the Bergen Line, attended their meetings. Many thousands of spectators would gather from far and near. A printed programme of competitors' names was published and at the event itself, the Scots were impressed to hear their names announced over a tannoy system for all to hear. Local newspapers treated it as an important occasion. In April of 1964, a party of 17 Scots went to Solfonn, in Norway to ski against a united team of Norwegians and Icelandics. On this occasion, they were accompanied by the new secretary, Guy Chilver-Stainer. The Scottish party were intrigued to watch the arrival of large quantities of paper sacks with "Kalk Saltpeter" written on the side. As Bob Benzies remembered at the time: "We took this to be calcium chloride, or something like it, but these bags were taken up and down the course and their contents sprinkled like grain from plastic buckets. It was then raked in, by a squad of forty men. Over the two days, they put down half a ton of the stuff and the effect was fantastic. Within half an hour, wet slush was transformed to hard snow with a good skiing grip on it, and this effect lasted for many hours without variation. Penalties for leaving the prepared course were, of course, greater, but each competitor skied the same course, and there was no question of deep ruts holding any of the late starters back."

The return visits of the Norwegians were as stimulating to the Scots as their journeys to Scandinavia. But by 1967, Jim Currie, the then President of the Scottish Ski Club, had to report that it had become increasingly difficult to raise an adequate team to send to Norway and with great reluctance the club decided to discontinue the meet. This had come about as the result of the improved competitions in Scotland and the greater emphasis on training, forcing teams to spend more time in the Alps.

One of the most memorable competitions to be held in Scotland was a ski instructors race organised on Cairngorm by Donnaie McKenzie. A few weeks before the race he had been in France and had met the new world champion, Charlot Bozon. To Donnaie's surprise the Frenchman accepted an invitation to ski in Scotland with alacrity. When news leaked out in Speyside that the champion was soon to be among them, the other competitors were horrified: "Bob Clyde, the chairlift Fuhrer, reported feverish slalom practice by the Austrians. The Norwegian ski school were exchanging top secret communiques with their own H.Q. in Oslo, which resulted in the arrival on the scene of one of their crack performers. The Canadian from the Badenoch Ski School, Austrians from Karl Fuch's stable, and one Swiss, were seen frantically training. The only Briton was Plum Worrall, working in Carrbridge. I cannot remember Coire na Ciste in better condition, and it was very satisfactory for the champ to find such snow for his visit to Scotland. His legs appeared to be made of high tensile spring steel, and his body capable of projecting itself into a forward to sideways position, which transferred effortlessly control of his skis. I began to wish in a way that he could hit some of the normal variety of vile Scottish crusted or wind slabbed corrugated surface, to see the champ's reactions. That will no doubt be available for his next visit."

The race itself was run down the "White Lady", the name given to the stretch of snow to the left of the chairlift, which previously had always been known as "Lady Grant". The new name seemed however to meet with more approval, and had now been generally accepted. The course was fast. Charlot Bozon won in 94.7 seconds, with the Norwegian second 0.2 seconds behind, Karl Fuchs was 9th, Hans Kuwall 12th and Plum, waving the flag for Britain, was number 20. This was Bozon's one and only visit to Scotland. The following year he was with a party of guides and students on his home ground above Chamonix, when a huge slab of snow became detached and carried the

Donnaie Mackenzie – an enthusiastic supporter of skiing in the Cairngorms. (Mackenzie Album)

whole party over a 3,000 foot drop into the Couloir. They were all killed.

Currency restrictions again proved a boost to Scottish skiing in 1967. They forced the British Alpine Ski Championships to be held in Scotland, rather than the Alps. Luckily by now the Cairngorm Winter Sports Board had increased the capacity of their upper chairlift and constructed a new White Lady ski tow. As the date for the competition drew near a blanket of snow completely covered the top of the mountain to the level of the Shieling.

The Times correspondent was most impressed with the organisation of the championships and was particularly enthusiastic with the commentary from Guy Chilver-Stainer which he broadcast from the roof of the chairlift station. Hamish Liddell was officially in charge of the championships, although as is reported in the Dundee Skiing Club journal: "Everybody seemed to have a title, and I do not mean the plethora of generals, majors, sirs or earls – I mean the chief of the course, the chief of the race, the chief of the equipment, the chief of gatekeepers and the three referees with every race – everybody was chief of something. We even had course police, who were entitled to marshal people and the reindeer, who got in the way." The highlight of the week's racing was the appearance of the successful British Ladies Team. Divina Galica and Georgina Hathorn skied in a manner that had not been seen in Scotland before.

This was the first race of any major importance to be held in Cairngorm. It was so successful that the Scottish Tourist Board and the Ski Federation of Great Britain hoped that it could come about more often. By the time the British Alpine Races returned to Scotland, the Cairngorm Winter Sports Development Board was able to declare that it now had a race course of internationally accepted standard. This had been put into effect by erecting 10,000 feet of fencing to the west of the White Lady Chairlift. Every international race course had now to be approved by the F.I.S. and areas wishing to have their course inspected had to prepare the necessary documents and apply for a qualified assessor who must be from another country, to examine the ground and determine whether or not the course was suitable.

On behalf of the F.I.S., Roland Rudin from Grindelwald, came to Cairngorm in the summer of 1971 to decide if the course could be "homologated". He had both to inspect the area and assess the adequacy of access, lifts, lodging facilities, shelter in the course area, snowfall, safety standards and communications between start and finish. He was satisfied and the Cairngorm Winter Sports Development Board was able to announce that they now had an international race course, starting some 500 metres due south of the chairlift top station, on the way to the summit, and finishing between the lower part of the nursery ski tow and the road. This meant that any races held by the National body on this course could now be included in the F.I.S. calendar, and so carry points on the world circuit, therefore attracting an international entry.

The Tourist Board's interest in skiing led to the Government publication of the report "The Cairngorm Area". This recommended new and better roads. The capital cost of the work suggested came to some thirty five million pounds. But, as the Secretary of State for Scotland, Mr William Ross remarked in the foreword "Neither the Government nor the local authorities who commissioned the survey, could be committed to this sort of money". One person who disagreed with the report was Stewart H. Anderson. He felt that a road was not the only means of access to a mountain area. He conducted his own survey for a railway instead. He proposed a monorail that would link Aviemore with Braemar through the Lairig Ghru. He explained his system in detail and insisted that when constructed it could carry 10,000 passengers per hour at a capital cost of £160,000 a mile.

Another innovator was not enthusiastic over Mr. Anderson's plan: "Mechanical devices are noisy and awkward and pulling an engine over hills can be a hideous pastime. Searching for a way to get the best of both worlds. I hit upon it. A parachute. The test flight took place on Carn Aosda in January during a south west gale. An R.A.F. parachute had been donated, fifteen feet in diameter, bright yellow, with sixteen nylon cords. Catching eight in each had, I flung the yellow bundle downwind, with ground crew gripping me tight to prevent a nose-over. Cotton billowed into life but the expected jerk did not materialise. Sad farewells and nervous giggles. A sudden gust, release and the top of Carn Aosda began to slide down to meet me. The one in two summit slope loomed up. A momentary pause, then the chute lifted and pulled violently. I felt something between ecstasy and panic as the summit cairn hurtled past. Thousands of rock teeth bared to repel the intruder. Enough. It works. Jettison a handful of cords. The chute convulsed to a writhing banner, while the wind, cheated of its victim, howled in frustration. Fumbling with numb hands, I dragged it into an army pack, then hunched up to get some speed against the gale. At the bottom once more, I looked up at the peak sparkling in the sun. I'd only one emotion – anticipation. Going up was almost as good as coming down."

It was said that a parachute was easier to handle than a rope tow, however one para-skier, Gordon McKay remembered that: "Only once did the parachute misbehave with me. An exceptionally strong gust full of ice particles hit me one day on the White Lady. I released one handful

Parachute skiing, first seen in Glenshee.
(Press and Journal)

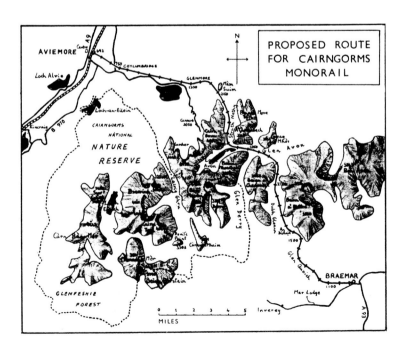

Proposal for a monorail link between
Aviemore and Braemar.
(Scottish Ski Club Journal)

of cords, as usual. Instead of streaming out in the wind, the chute rose like some weird aerofoil, suspended me, puppet-like from the cords I still held." Mr. McKay remarked that slaloming through crowded slopes was tricky, as people did not seem to appreciate being enveloped by a parachute, particularly when wet.

Perhaps it was this bizarre parachute skiing which sparked off the idea of the first "Highland Pentathlon". This event was conceived by Captain John Wells, the then manager of the new Aviemore centre. It was to be a blend of skiing, swimming, shooting and running. The competitors in teams of three were drawn from Scottish Universities, clubs and the Services, and sponsored by John Player. As it happened, the skiers were worse at the curling than the latter were at skiing, and were both equally bad at shooting, compared with the Service competitors, whose team won the event.

The intention of the first Highland Pentathlon was to underline the fact that the new Aviemore centre was open and in operation. This development had cost £2,500,000, and was a complex of hotels, chalets and entertainment facilities, attached to what, up until now, had been the small village of Aviemore. It was to have a tremendous impact on the Spey Valley. With the extra attractions of indoor ice rink, swimming pool, cinema, dance hall, bowling alley and shops, it was the first place in Scotland that came anywhere near the continental idea of a "resort".

A young Austrian from Solbad Hall near Innsbruck, moved to Scotland at this time. Leopold Vielhaber came from a family of ski makers. He came to Britain to learn English but married a Scots girl and instead of returning home, set up a business for himself at Birnam in Perthshire. His aim was to manufacture a range of fibreglass skis especially designed to give good service under Scottish conditions. His first skis were known as Comet and came in three grades, ranging in price from £26 to £45. Guy Chilver-Stainer was invited to test the new Vielhaber skis and he reported that he was most impressed with their performance.

The English D.H.O. Ski Club commissioned Leo Vielhaber to produce a genuine junior racer ski, with an accurately scaled down profile. At the same time the British Ski Team accepted a set of his second model, the Ambassador, that had a hardwearing plastic heel. Later, Leo Vielhaber was to introduce a carbon fibre ski, thus endorsing his advertisement "We make the tracks, other follow."

There was certainly a market in Scotland for a versatile ski. Schools all over the country realised that skiing had a place in their curriculum. As the Head of the Physical Education Department of Aberdeen said at the time: "Skiing is a sport where one is self-dependent. It brings health,

self-assurance and contentment. Moreover, in Aberdeen it is financially within the means of everyone". Aberdeen was the first Education Authority in Scotland to buy skis and boots for the use of its pupils. It arranged a ten week course with professional instruction. Between New Year and Easter buses full of children and teachers would leave the city every Saturday and head for the snow. Edinburgh Corporation was close behind Aberdeen and by the end of the 60's, was able to say that they had introduced thousands of schoolchildren to the snow via the plastic slope at Hillend.

More skiers meant crowded ski slopes, long cold waits for lifts and tows and delays on access roads. More people were talking of alternative areas to be opened up for skiing. Benn Wyvis and Aonach Mor were discussed, each area having its own band of enthusiasts who declared that their plans were furtherest on and their site the most ideal. Both, in fact, were handicapped by poor access. In 1968, the Loch Rannoch Hotel at Kinlochrannoch, provided two tractor operated continuous rope tows for its clients. The Dalmunzie Hotel, not to be outdone installed a bobsleigh run to entertain skiers fed up with standing in queues. One competitor remembers the first championships to be held on this course: "The first tentative runs down the course were taken at moderate speed, complicated only by the degree of intoxication of the runner. However, as the course speeded up, so did the spirits motivating the runners. The fastest time of the day was turned in by Allan Christie, who, failing to negotiate the right-hander at the foot of the run, actually got half way across the river, before he sank with a great degree of skill. Jim 'Beef' Gellatly made a number of dashing runs, proceeding at one point on one runner, poised above the river for some yards. However, by adjusting his weight, he fell back the right way, to the audible disappointment of the onlookers".

At the end of the decade there were tows in many areas and new huts belonging to the Scottish Ski Club in both the Cairngorms and Glenshee. A propos of more development in the hills, Captain Ian Tennant said 'Let us be sure that this great sport of skiing remains a sport and never becomes a battle''.

Leo Vielhaber, he started making fibre glass skis at Birnam in 1968. (M.R. Kenneth)

Fixing the skis onto the helicopter below
Ben Alder.
(M.R. Kenneth)

A touring party of the Scottish Ski Club
was engulfed by an avalanche above the
Lairig Ghru.
(H. Simpson)

12. OUTER LIMITS

Birgitte Single of West Germany competing in the Europa Cup Grass Championships held at Hillend in 1977. (M.R. Kenneth)

The seventies saw several new developments in skiing. Grass skiing was one of these. Large caterpillar-type roller skates had been invented in Germany. They could be used on any reasonably smooth grass slope of moderate gradient and could be manoeuvred to turn. Aerolyne Plastics Ltd. provided the Scottish Ski Club with grass skis and these were tested for the first time at Amulree in October 1970. This summertime sport took a few years to really catch on, but interest was aroused with the news that the Italian ski team were using grass skis for summer training.

A few of the racers who frequented Hillend became enthusiastic. They felt that the movements of grass skiing were closer to "real" skiing than those on the plastic slope. Meanwhile, a system of races emerged in England. The Hillend Scots immediately began to compete and quickly reached prominence in the finish lists. In 1975, one of the national events in the British calendar was held at Hillend. Short, sheep-cropped grass at the site of the artificial slope was ideal for this new sport, the only exception being a large number of gorse bushes dotted about the hill. One fall into these and the skier either became proficient overnight or gave up the sport.

When asked "What was it like to grass ski?" one enthusiast, Carolann Beck, answered: "Well, balancing three inches up on moving platforms two feet long and two inches wide is difficult, at least for the first few runs. Good skiers, however, pick it up quickly. The main stumbling block, apart from balance, is the lack of the skid element in turning. Any attempt at unweighting and skidding results in green knees and stained trousers. Grass-skis are much more positive than their snow counterparts although the same basic movements are used. Turns are executed on the inside edge, they can be made faster by leaning back and accelerating the skis forward when coming out of a turn although this results in a muddy posterior for the first few times."

Skiers have always looked for ways of increasing the length of their season. One method was to charter a helicopter and so reach residual snow lying close to the summit. Bob Clyde was the first to use this means of uplift to ski in Scotland. A close second was Bob Benzies. He chartered a machine to take him to the summit of Lochnagar in April of 1972. It was a four-seater from Kestrel Helicopters and the pilot, John Poland, picked him up along with three companions a 9 a.m. from the front lawn of Dalmunzie Hotel in Glenshee. The flight to the summit took 15 minutes, the snow was in excellent condition and the skiers had a memorable run down, rejoining the helicopter which had landed within 200 yards of a herd of deer, who were completely unperturbed.

Their experience inspired Mike Kenneth to follow suit the following year. He chose the Ben Alder area and selected a perfect day. The helicopter picked up his party of four at Dalwhinnie. One of them, Dick West, remembers that: "We put down on an almost snow-free ridge, some 150 feet below Ben Alder summit. We were left to absolute peace and wonderful views, with visibility of 60 odd miles in every direction. And so on ski, down fine open slopes of genuine powder snow for 450 feet, then some circumspect skiing round broken rock outcrops for a couple of hundred feet. This bit was extraordinarily Alpine in character, and was followed by a spring snow schuss to the bealach. Here the snow was still frozen and gave us a splendid, easy zig-zag to the edge of the blue-green ice of the loch. We had had 6,000 feet of superb skiing, a leisurely lunch beside the frozen loch, had visited three of the remoter peaks of Scotland and enjoyed some of the clearest views we had ever seen. Small wonder then, at my shock when I looked at my watch on return. It was only half past three! What couldn't one do in a whole day of 'copter skiing". Bureaucracy and conservationists closed in however and few others have since had the experience of helicopter skiing in Scotland.

The traditions of Allan Arthur, Harry MacRobert and the other early tourers were still maintained by members of the Scottish Ski Club, with a crossing of the Cairngorms every Easter. In 1975 this event went badly wrong. The nine man tour began at Achlean in Glen Feshie. Conditions were ideal. Continuous falls of snow meant that they could put on their touring skis at the car-park. They skinned up to the Great Moss, then schussed through the lip of Glen Geuschagan down to the river flats. This served as an easy route, being largely covered with snow. Turning into the Devil's Point, towards Corrour, they met a fierce head-on blizzard. However, the men eventually reached the warm security of the bothy and set out again next day in perfect conditions. The Lairig floor was a carpet of snow and a steady rhythm soon had the party lunching in bright sunshine on the summit. They now had to find an easy access route to the Macdhui Plateau. Glancing up at the steepening sides it seemed that there was a route in one of the many gullies that broke the Lairig steepness at the crest.

The party climbed first on rocks, preferring to carry skis because of the steepness. One hundred feet from the top the main body of the party noticed that the one on the snow was making better progress than themselves. They followed suit, then suddenly became aware of the whole slab of snow beginning to move downhill. Fractions of a second later they lost their footing and were immediately covered in snow and gasping for breath. Down and down they tumbled, with an agonising banging as their bodies hit rocks and boulders. Upside down, skis and rucksacks pulling in all directions. Then at last the movement stopped. One of the victims remembers: "I could see Graham Boyd 30 yards away. As I watched his white jersey went crimson with blood. It was a desperate struggle to get on my feet. Limbs felt leaden. Looking over the avalanche fall, 7 bodies were strewn out, broken and bent skis, sticks, rucksacks and other equipment littered the hill." Two of the party were able to ski out for assistance and soon the injured were being winched up by an R.A.F. helicopter, which had them quickly in hospital at Inverness.

Crowded ski slopes encouraged the tourers to set off into the hills. Other, younger skiers found an alternative was to make more use of the available snow. A type of skiing evolved, known in America as "hot-dogging". Freestyle, as it was later termed came about because the increased crowds, using short skis, caused large bumps to form on the snow. Out of this came a competition, consisting of three parts for which points were awarded, as in ice skating, ballet, free-style skiing over "moguls", and aerial acrobatics.

The first competition in Scotland was promoted by Harp Lager and more spectators appeared on the scene than at any other ski event yet held. The exhuberant enthusiasm of the hot-doggers was infectious. After a competition, junior racers and students could be seen borrowing shovels and erecting mini-jumps. Such activity had not been seen on Scottish snow since the 1920s when the Scottish Ski Club had considered that every ski slope should have a jumping platform. Soon the emphasis on free-style moved towards mogul runs and parallel slaloms. For most skiers, these events were closer to the essence of the sport, the mobility and freedom of skiing fast over any terrain with confidence. It was as if the modern young skier was searching for that freedom of the hills that Naismith, Harry MacRobert and Willie Spiers enjoyed in the early days.

The exhilaration that could be found in the hills was being experienced by a continually widening group of people. Even the physically handicapped were finding the joys that could be had from the snow.

Hotdogging on Cairngorm. A new way to make use of limited snow and also to extend one's ability.
(H. Simpson)

Norman Piercy uses his "outriggers" to negotiate a turn on Cairngorm, 1978. (M.R. Kenneth)

Norman Piercy had lost his leg when 21 and did not start to ski until he was 46. He was driven to learning to ski by the boredom of waiting for his family to return from the snow in Glenshee. He hated the sport however until he encountered an American doctor who told him of the many Vietnam veterans who had learned to ski on one leg, using a single ski and outriggers in either hand. He urged Norman to have another try. Norman remembers that: "I felt reluctant, but as I thought of the bright happy faces of my skiing family, and how much they seemed to enjoy it, I resolved at least to have a go... I was introduced to Derek Brightman, ski instructor for Cairdsport, Aviemore, who gave the impression that instructing unfit middle-aged, one legged skiers, who had never skied in their lives before, just happened to him every day. He was quite unflappable and so very relaxed, which was just as well, for I began to have misgivings, especially when we decided that I would have to go up in the chair. My progress was rather slow and at times I felt that I would never manage to ski, but with Derek's encouragement and mild bullying, I slowly began to get the message... The first long traverse that I did without falling, was a wonderful experience. As my balance improved I was actually able to lift both my outriggers as I sailed along on the single ski."

Norman Piercy wanted to hand on his confidence to other disabled skiers, but felt that in order to help them, he must learn to instruct properly and so in May 1976, he took the B.A.S.I. course. To his great delight, he passed the grade three qualification. He now urges all who consider themselves disabled, to adopt this "wonderful sport, where they will find happiness in fitness."

With the organised ski areas crowded by hot-doggers, handicapped or modified skiers, parachutists, school children, racers as well as the normal ski enthusiasts, there was a clear need for long term planning to ease the congestion. To establish priorities the Highland Regional Council commissioned a survey. A group of ski experts, familiar with the Highlands, was assembled and taken by helicopter to every potential ski area. The leader of the group was Eric Langmuir, a former principal of Glenmore Lodge and a B.A.S.I. grade one ski instructor. The other members were Bob Clyde, Guy Chilver-Stainer, Clive Freshwater, a qualified teacher and B.A.S.I. trainer, David Patterson, general manager of the Glenshee ski area for 16 years, and Jack Thomson of Glenmore Lodge.

The report divided the mountains into three categories for potential development: small scale; large scale; and major complex. Among the small scale developments, it was considered that A'chailleach to the west of Newtonmore, had the most potential, being an extensive, open slope

David Mercer competing in the British
Championships held on Cairngorm,
April 1980.
(M.R. Kenneth)

Lesley Beck competing in the Hird
Trophy in March 1980. This is the
slalom event in the Scottish Ski Club
Championships.
(M.R. Kenneth)

suitable for beginners. Next in line, the group decided, was Drumochter, with a succession of more than a dozen narrow, V-shaped gullies mainly with one run in each but with gradients suitable for intermediate skiers. Third they suggested that Aonach Mor, two miles to the north of Fort William, would provide suitable snow for good and intermediate skiers. For large scale developments, the survey team considered that there was much untapped potential in Glencoe, secondly, that Creag Meagaidh, with two large, south facing corries and related gullies, offered a great variety of skiing for about 4,000 skiers at any one time. Third in line of the large scale developments, the group considered that Ben Wyvis could provide skiing mainly for beginners and intermediates, in the single large, south-facing bowl, with perhaps one or two adjacent runs in mid winter.

The main emphasis of the survey was on the group's assessment of the most suitable sites for a major ski complex, and here they considered that without doubt, Braeriach offered the best potential in Scotland. It had eight large snow fields, discharging into numerous gullies, leading down to Glen Einich. They regarded this as the best all round downhill ski area, in terms of the variety and length of runs. Between January and March, they considered that up to three miles of downhill skiing were possible and that the area had an estimated ski capacity well in excess of 10,000. Access would have to be from Glen Einich. Considering Cairngorm, the team decided that the three main snow fields were already developed to capacity but that external expansion was possible into a further four corries, adjoining these snow-fields. Coire Laogh Mor to the east and to the west, Coire an t'Sneachda, Coire an Lochain and Lurcher's Gully. The whole of this western area could be serviced from a single access road. The present development has a skiing capacity of 5,000 when in full operation, but expansion to the new areas would add a further 5,000 to this.

The group also came to the conclusion that there was considerable potential in Glenshee. They suggested that more tows could be erected on the east of Meall-Odhar, in two very large adjoining snow fields. The existing skiing area had a capacity of nearly 3,000, which could be expanded to another 500 with these further developments. They also drew attention to the fact that expansion east into Ghlas Choire and the Garbh Choire, would bring the total ski capacity to about 7,000.

The Langmuir survey maintained that it made good sense to capitalise on existing investments where there was spare capacity instead of breaking new ground. It stated that the further development of a ski area involved providing the right balance of facilities that included slope improvement, shelter, refreshment and toilets, and building them all in such a way as to harmonise with the mountain setting and cause the minimum of damage to the environment.

There is something for all skiers in the Scottish hills, from the intrepid ski mountaineer to the raw beginner. The wheel has turned and there is at the moment an exodus outward towards the remote, rarely visited places and gullies. The trend is called "ski extreme" and is a search for the same goal sought by the skisters of the past. Jim Harrison, editor of the Scottish Ski Club Journal, perhaps explains why, "Ski touring for me has been a lifelong lesson in humility. That extra mile has often been unobtainable, that mastery of technique beyond grasp, that breakthrough into broad and sunlit upland of assured and confident style never comes. Why then keep trying? Why keep battling winter after winter with the uncertainties of Scottish weather? Companionship is undoubtedly part of it all. There is a mystic bond forged among the hills. ... Just as companionship may be part of it all, the desire to explore hill country, to find the best route which will give one the longest downhill running, is also a part of the challenge of ski touring and just to pause on the way up, warm in the early spring sun, is a pleasure which one cannot earn in merely carrying a deck chair to a sheltered spot in the garden."

From tweed clad "skisters" alone on trackless snow to colourful crowds on mogulled pistes, Scottish skiing has changed greatly. But the essence of enjoying the high mountain environment in all weathers still remains. Allan Arthur warned against ski fever. To some, this may be looked upon as a dreaded plague to be avoided. To others, it is the doorway to an exhilarating new way of life.

INDEX

R. WYLIE HILL & CO., LTD.
GLASGOW

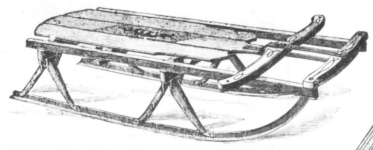

The "Flexible Flyer." A Self-Steering Sledge.

Length 36 ins., Price 13/6.   Length 40 ins., Price 17/6.

As Illustrated.

Length 45 ins., Price 23/6.   Length 50 ins., Price 28/6.

,,   62 ins.,   ,,   34/6.   ,,   101 ins.,   ,,   57/6.

The "Fire-Fly." A Self-Steering Sledge.

Length 36 ins., Price 10/6.

,,   40 ins.,   ,,   13/6.

,,   45 ins.,   ,,   17/6.

SLEDGES

The Clipper Sledge.
Fitted with Round Spring Shoes.

Length 36 ins., Price 8/6.

,,   40 ins.,   ,,   10/6.

,,   44 ins.,   ,,   13/6.

Our Boys' Sledge.
Round Iron Shoes.

Length 30, 33, 40 ins.

Price   2/9, 3/9, 5/9.

Length 44 ins.

Price 6/6.

Youths'.
6 ft., 34/6 Pair.

Ladies'.
6 ft. 6 in., 35/6 Pair.

Gents'.
7 ft., 36/6 Pair.

7 ft 3 ins., 37/6 Pair.

Ski Wax (Hard).
1/- per Tablet, postage 3d. extra.

Ski Wax (Soft).
1/- per Tube, postage 3d. extra.

Ski Oil.
6d. per Tin, postage 3d. extra.

Ski Sticks.
3/- and 4/- each.

SNOW SKI

Real Canadian Toboggans.

4 ft.	5 ft.	6 ft.	7 ft.	8 ft. Long.
18/6.	21/6.	25/6.	31/6.	35/6. Price.